THREE CENTURIES AT KAWSMOUTH

The French Foundations of Metropolitan Kansas City

BY

CHARLES E. HOFFHAUS

THE LOWELL PRESS / KANSAS CITY

TO

THE

MEMORY

OF MY MOTH-

ER, WHO TAUGHT

ME TO LOVE THE CITY

OF MY BIRTH, AND OF MY

COUSIN, ENOS A. MILLS, FATHER

OF THE ROCKY MOUNTAIN NATIONAL

PARK, WHOSE BOOKS AND FAMILY LEG-

ENDS INSPIRED IN ME AN APPRECIATION

OF THE BEAUTY AND HISTORY OF THE WEST,

AND TO

VEDA, STACY AND SUSAN

Contents

Illustrations

Acknowledgments

AT THE PALACE OF VERSAILLES, in late August, 1969, I sat looking out over the artificial lagoon beyond the formal gardens to the two huge poplars in the hazy distance at the far end of the palace grounds. This inspiring view seemed to stretch on to the ends of the earth, just as the power emanating from this palace did in its heyday. I was struck by the thought that, in the late 1600s and the 1700s, there were people living there who could and did give orders which made things happen in the future Kansas City! They could build forts, buy beaver furs, mount expeditions, reward friendly chiefs, or change post commandants. This was rather like looking through the wrong end of a telescope, and things in that era admittedly seemed on a rather lilliputian scale in Kansas City compared to the great doings at Versailles. But even though the future Kansas City was no Versailles, it is of vast interest to us that, 150 years *before* our more familiar cowboys and Indians type of history even started, people like Louis XIV, Louis XV, John Law, and Madame de Pompadour were taking a vital interest in our area. I had written articles on French colonial subjects and on that summer day at Versailles, *voilà*, the idea came into focus that some day I might try to organize my research into a book.

My main source of French colonial information was the Kansas City Public Library, especially the very fine Missouri Valley Room. The second source, several years ago before the materials were deposited with the Kansas City Public Library, was the Archives of the Native Sons of Kansas City—which really means the late James Anderson. As Ted Brown rightly pointed out in his *Frontier Community—Kansas City to 1870*, "all serious work on Kansas City's history must begin with a visit to him." He wrote and talked enthusiastically about the French, and it was catching. He once told me that he visited as a young man in the Kansas City, Kansas, home of a son or grandson of Mr. Philibert, the old Kansa Indian agent, and overheard several elderly gentlemen there speaking French! I must also acknowledge my debt to the inexhaustible files of the Missouri Historical Society in St. Louis and to the Loudon Collection of the Huntington Library at San Marino, California.

I would also like to pay my respects to a bright spirit whose enthusiasm kindled my own and was also to a considerable degree responsible for this book. Blanche Chouteau (whose married name was Brecklein), a great-great-great-granddaughter of Rene Auguste Chouteau, the co-founder of St. Louis, though in her ninety-fifth year when I first made her acquaintance, was darkly beautiful and ever so proud of her Gallic antecedents and delighted to talk about them. Her grandfather was Paul Liguest ("Major") Chouteau, and her father was Auguste Liguest Chouteau. She heard her father speak often of his uncles, François (founder of Kansas City) and C. G. Chouteau. More fascinating to me was the fact that she knew and spoke affectionately and at length of her great-aunt (and François' widow) Madame Berenice Chouteau—the French grande dame of Kansas City until her death in 1888. Blanche was about 24 then. Blanche said she was "the last of the Chouteaus" in Kansas City. Her reminiscences, told with keen eye and ready wit (and cut all too short by a traumatic change in her health resulting from a fall from her bed), convinced me that others, too, would enjoy learning about the French background of the area around Kawsmouth.

In this book, which stops where others start, I have undertaken the work of a pathfinder and I gladly accept responsibility for any errors or shortcomings. If I am so fortunate as to have a second printing I hope to rectify any shortfalls and add any new material which may be called to my attention by interested readers.

I acknowledge the kind permission of the following publications to reprint material which first appeared in their pages: Kansas Historical Society *Quarterly* (on Fort Cavagnial), The Kansas City *Star* (on Fort Cavagnial, de Bourgmont and Lewis and Clark) and the *UMKC Law Journal* (on the Custom of Paris). Bruce Mathews provided the photographs on pages xvi, 91, 165 and 189. I extend particular thanks to my secretary, Rhonda Dennis, who typed (and retyped) the manuscript on the magic word processor, to my very competent friends at The Lowell Press, The Chouteau Society, and my law partners who indulged my whim to go to press.

CHARLES E. HOFFHAUS

Letter from Pierre Chouteau, Jr., to C. G. Chouteau at Chez les Canses dated August 30, 1820. Courtesy of Missouri Historical Society.

Introduction

THE CENTENNIAL SPANNING the period from the founding of Fort de Cavagnial (north of present Ft. Leavenworth) in 1744 to the great Missouri River flood of 1844 is an historical hiatus for most Kansas Citians, yet it marked a colorful and well-recorded era of more or less permanent French-speaking settlement of our region. In fact, Kansas City's French history can fairly be said to have started with an event which happened 600 miles away and three centuries ago, in 1680. In that year the pueblos at Taos and elsewhere in New Mexico revolted against the Spanish, causing them to retreat in a panic to the Southwest and creating a void into which the French traders stepped in increasing numbers, coming up the Missouri (where two of them were detained by the Missouri Indians in 1680) to Kawsmouth, and across the plains to Taos and Santa Fe.

This book was a labor of love—the result of my efforts to trace the earliest historical roots of my home town, which, we tend to forget, started as a French enclave in the Western wilderness. The fact that many of the sources useful in the preparation of this book were in French presented a challenge, but not a particularly disagreeable one. The combination of the language problem and our excusable Anglophilic myopia make it considerably more difficult to find easily accessible colonial and post-colonial materials dealing with our area than would be the case, say, with the Eastern Seaboard.

The colonial history of metropolitan Kansas City—and there is an abundance of such history—was *French* colonial history, with just a dash of Spanish colonial history thrown in. The original colonial materials are usually in St. Louis, New Orleans, Montreal, Quebec, or Paris (into each of whose voluminous archives I have delved); and the early post-colonial materials are scattered, fragmentary, and poorly recorded.

Our area was the focus for colonial action in major Franco-Spanish and Franco-British wars. We had a Regency period fort, Fort Orleans named after the Regent, and a Louis XV fort, Fort de Cavagnial, both following the classic design of Marshal Vauban. Our area did millions of livres of business in the fur trade a century before the Santa Fe Trail, and even *that* was started by the French in the early 1700s on their annual trading trips to the Taos Fair and Santa Fe.

The etymology of the name Kansas City bears mention. The name *Kanzas* or *Kanses* was applied to the French post and colony at the Kansa grand village north of Fort Leavenworth in the mid 1700s and the name *Canses* or *Cansez* (abbreviated as Cans.) among others was also applied to the French-speaking settlement (or town if you will) in the old French Bottoms where the stockyards are now situated. So were the names *Chez les Canses* (meaning "home" or "village" of the Kansa) and *Chouteau's*. This settlement formed the nucleus for the later development of the entire metropolitan Kansas City area, becoming in natural sequence after Village of the Kansa, the Town of Kansas, the City of Kansas, then "Kansas City." It is this greater metropolitan area, extending out for perhaps 70 miles, to which I refer in this book whenever I use the term *Kansas City*.

Etienne Veniard, Sieur de Bourgmont. Detail from panorama by Daniel MacMorris, courtesy of Missouri Valley Room of Kansas City Public Library.

CHAPTER I

Missi Sepe and Pekitanoui

IN THE BAS-RELIEF FRIEZE sculptured on the east face of Kansas City, Missouri City Hall is a scene depicting, in heroic-sized figures, an eighteenth century French officer (de Bourgmont), his aide, a standard bearing the lilies of the Bourbon *ancien régime* of France, and two Indians. Over the librarian's desk in the Missouri Valley Room of the Kansas City, Missouri Public Library is a panorama by Daniel MacMorris, showing this same Frenchman, his entourage, and the Indians on high ground overlooking the Missouri River somewhere in the Kansas City area. De Bourgmont and the French settlement surrounding Chouteau's post at Kawsmouth for years provided the lead-in paragraphs (albeit somewhat inaccurate) for the capsule history of Kansas City in the Kansas City Telephone Directory.

Who were these Frenchmen? Were they simply the result of artistic license designed to inject a romantic image into a local history surfeited with abattoirs? Could they possibly have been here in the early 1700s? The answer is a definite and resounding *yes*—they were here, probably as early as the 1690s, and they explored, mapped, and named our rivers and streams; named and civilized the Indian tribes in our area; and started the first commerce of the Kansas City region—furs. They brought with them their language, religion, and system of law: vestiges of all three survive to this day. In the final epoch of their fur-trading enterprises there arose at Chouteau's post a *centre de la ville* around which gravitated a handful of French

1

traders and farmers—the nucleus of present-day metropolitan
Kansas City. The original site of the town company of the
Town of Kansas was platted on the farm of one of them,
Gabriel Prudhomme. It is my purpose to tell their story.

That story will take us back more than a century and
one-half before the original town company of Kansas City,
Missouri, was formed and will trace the history of our area as it
became, successively, a geographical nameplace and landmark
on the Missouri River route, a rendezvous for coureurs de bois,
a fur-trading station, and finally a farming settlement—all
distinctively French.

It is occasionally suggested that the Kansas City region
remained virtually *terra incognita* until the French founded St.
Louis, after which time our area was developed for the first
time as a part of the St. Louis hinterland. This is not altogether
accurate and is unnecessarily demeaning. It was our much-
traversed hinterland that made possible the virtual overnight
birth of St. Louis. Starting as early as the 1690s and increas-
ingly from 1700 on, the Missouri River area to the east and
north of Kawsmouth was the center of a vast and ever-growing
two-way traffic in furs and French trade goods. This was more
than one-half century before St. Louis' founding in 1765,
during which time the immediate site of present St. Louis was
pristine wilderness.

Geographical conditions made Kawsmouth a natural stop-
ping place in this trade, while the same was not true of the St.
Louis riverbank site. The latter (although not far from the
mouth of the Missouri) was picked by Laclede more or less at
random from miles of virtually identical terrain in either
direction up or down the Mississippi. The area immediately
adjacent to the mouth of the Kaw, on the other hand, formed
an unmistakable and well-known landmark where trading
parties and Indians could and did rendezvous; goods could be
traded for furs on the spot, segregated and cached, or trans-
shipped for the Kaw or the upper Missouri; and traders' furs
from both sources could be collected and stored for down-

stream shipment. One large-scale trader, Avion, even an-
ticipated present Kansas City by a century by setting up shop
among the Kansa at or near Kawsmouth in 1752. The
principal French settlements during this period were on the
Illinois side of the Mississippi, at Kaskaskia, Cahokia, St.
Phillipe, and Fort de Chartres. The only trading station on the
west side of the river in the Illinois region (unless the River des
Peres mission could be so dignified) was at Ste. Genevieve,
much lower down than the future St. Louis site.

The future Kansas City environs were the most prolific
source of the highest grade of beaver furs so much in demand
in Europe. The European trade goods coming upriver consisted of tools, cloth, weapons, beads, trinkets—and occasionally
liquor. A full-scale French trading depot was in existence for
twenty years, from 1744 to 1764, within what many (including
the Kansas City Chamber of Commerce) consider the ambit of
the present-day Kansas City metropolitan area. This was the
Kansa Indian trading post at Fort de Cavagnial located just
north of Ft. Leavenworth, Kansas. This emporium was the
direct lineal antecedent (by way of a series of licensed resident
Kansa traders) of a later Kansa (or "Canses") trading station,
Chouteau's store near Kawsmouth, which formed the nucleus
for present-day Kansas City. All this trade over the decades
built up an unquenchable head of furs flowing downriver and
an insatiable market for trade goods flowing upriver. This
trade extended from Fort de Chartres, at the Illinois, up the
Missouri to the Platte, and Kawsmouth and the region around
it formed the midway point astride this established trade
route. Trade goods up in the fall—furs down in the spring—this
cycle went on without interruption year after year from the
1690s on. St. Louis sprang full-blown into a city after its
founding in 1765 because it was the sole successor to Fort de
Chartres as the downstream entrepôt of this ready-made and
extremely lucrative system of trade. The long-established
upstream collection system flowing past (and at times center-
ing in) the ancient French rendezvous at Chez les Canses,

which became Kansas City, went on as before—only the eastern terminus was new.

The story really begins, as all must which deal with early-day exploration of the New World, with geography—the· lay of the land. The central geographical fact of the entire mid-America area, from the Appalachians to the Rockies, is the Mississippi River and its vast system of tributaries— principal among which is, of course, the Missouri. The first parts of this story are in essence a narrative of the attempts of a few intrepid Franco-Europeans to traverse a part of this tremendous tract of real estate for the first time and establish a few points of reference therein.

To the modern-day traveler accustomed to heading for Kansas City on Interstate 70 from St. Louis or western Kansas, points of reference mean little—all you have to do is keep going, and you can't miss. You know where you want to go and you know the highway will take you there. But the early-day explorers had (except for vague reports from the Indians) no conception of where their travels might lead them, nor any idea of what they might find at their "destination." At the risk of belaboring the obvious, let us take a brief look at the topography which these explorers covered in order to appreciate their reports and also for the benefit of those not personally familiar with the area.

The Mississippi divides the intermountain midlands roughly in half, flowing from Minnesota south to the Gulf of Mexico. Its eastern tributaries, which are numerous, do not concern us here. About midway between its source in the north and its mouth in the gulf, several miles above St. Louis, Missouri, the Missouri River empties in on the west side. The Missouri's course is roughly in a line from west to east from Kansas City to St. Louis. But at Kansas City the river makes an abrupt turn to the north, and its course from there on is essentially to the north, and in North Dakota and Montana, to the west again.

Right at the big bend where the Missouri turns to the north at Kansas City, the Kansas or Kaw River (or *Canses* as the

French called it) enters the Missouri. Although it crosses the eastern part of Kansas in a roughly west to east direction, the Kansas River actually enters the Missouri from the southwest after skirting around an area of bottomland between its (the Kaw's) east bank and the bluffs still further to the east. It is upon these river bluffs that downtown Kansas City, Missouri, is now situated. A small stream, Turkey Creek (its course considerably modified in recent years), flows into the Kansas River at the southern end of this bottomland. The low-lying area is identified today as the Central Industrial District and is the site of the Kansas City Stockyards, the remains of several large packing houses, railyards, and various industrial establishments. Of this general area at "Kawsmouth," the bottomland from Turkey Creek to the Missouri, and its eastern extension around the bluffs to the Chouteau Bridge, I shall have more to say later. It was there, in the old French Bottoms, that Kansas City had its genesis.

The discovery, exploration, and early settlement of the Missouri River—and of the metropolitan Kansas City area in particular—were exclusively the accomplishment of the French. Louis XIV, the "Sun King," who epitomized the climax of the greatest period of development in French history, was probably more responsible than anyone else for the ultimate discovery and exploitation of the Kansas City area. He dreamed of founding a colonial empire in North America which would rival that of Spain—and his slightest wishes were veritable commands. When he came to power in 1658, New France was confined to the valley of the St. Lawrence River, and the Mississippi had not been seen by any Frenchman. Before his death, through the efforts (which he inspired) of Colbert, Talon, Frontenac, Marquette and Joliet, La Salle, Tonty, Bourgmont, Le Sueur, and others like them, the French had explored both the Mississippi and the Missouri. Indeed, de Bourgmont in 1713, two years before Louis XIV's death, had conducted a detailed survey of the Missouri to the Platte, describing clearly the area at Kawsmouth and camped on the site of present Kansas City, Missouri, en route. But this is getting ahead of our story.

Jacques Cartier may have faintly fathomed the vastness of the land to the west when in 1535 he stood on the summit of Mont-Real (presently Montreal, Canada) looking westward up the St. Lawrence and listened to the accounts of the savages regarding the surrounding lands and waters. Samuel de Champlain, sent in 1603 by a company of French merchants to survey the potential of the St. Lawrence, and returning frequently thereafter (finally becoming governor of the new colony), caught a vision of the potentiality of the West when the Indians drew a crude map for him of the St. Lawrence and the lakes and rivers beyond. Champlain early heard from the Indians (probably the Ottawas whom he met in 1615 and whose tribe traded annually as far westward as the Rockies) of a "Great Water" to the west, which we now know as the Mississippi and its tributaries. Champlain looked upon it as a possible short route to China and made it his policy to learn all he could about it.

In 1618 he engaged a promising youth, Jean Nicolet, to learn the languages of the more remote tribes of savages to the west to the end that he might act as guide, diplomat, and interpreter in order to further Champlain's plans for westward discovery. In late June, 1634, Nicolet set out to the West on a voyage designed to cement relations with and among the western tribes, develop trade, and discover, if possible, the Great Water Route to Asia. In fragile birchbark canoes, Nicolet and his party wended their way up the St. Lawrence, through the Great Lakes via the falls of the St. Marys River (Sault St. Marie), up Green Bay, the Fox River and Lake Winnebago to the lands of the Mascoutins in present-day Wisconsin. There he heard from the Indians of the Wisconsin River (only three days distant) and of a *missi sepe* (Algonquin for "great river") connected with the same, leading to the sea. Nicolet erroneously interpreted this to mean he was on the verge of the western ocean leading to Asia. His reports upon his return to the St. Lawrence probably constituted the first recorded descriptions of the French regarding the Mississippi, its tributaries, and its course to the Gulf of Mexico. The *Jesuit Relations* for the year 1640 says that "Le Sieur Nicolet" penetrated to within three days of "un grand fleuve qui sort de ce lac, qu'il auroit trouve la mer." This report gave rise to a burning desire on the part of the Jesuits to find an easy way via the Mississippi or its tributaries to the western sea—a desire which, as we shall see, motivated Père Marquette until his death—and which was not laid to rest until the expedition of Lewis and Clark.

The Spanish (perhaps because of De Soto's and Coronado's explorations) and through them eventually the English and French early learned of the river route from northeastern New Mexico to the St. Lawrence. This route probably extended overland to the Platte, down the Missouri (past the site of present Kansas City), and up the Mississippi, Wisconsin, and Fox rivers to the Great Lakes. The following from the *Jesuit Relations* for 1660 is a sample of the information then extant:

> The twenty-fourth day of June (1660), there arrived an Englishman, with a servant, brought in boats by twenty Abnaquiois savages. . . . He told us wonderful things of New Mexico. "I learned," said he, "that one can sail to that country by means of the seas [i.e., large lakes and rivers] which lie to the north of it. . . ." We have strong indications that one can descend through the second lake of the Hurons [i.e., Lake Michigan and Green Bay] and through the country of the nations we have named [in the *Relations* of the Nicolet voyage] into the sea [Mississippi-Missouri, et al.] which he was trying to find.

Within recent years there were discovered in the Bodleian Library at Oxford University and promptly published the manuscripts of the explorations of a remarkable Frenchman, Pierre Esprit Radisson. One of his journeys is of particular interest to us. In the spring of 1659 two adventurers, Radisson

and his brother-in-law Groseilliers, embarked on their "southern" journey. This took them into some part of the country
where according to Radisson "it never snows nor freezes there,
but mighty hot." While on this trip they discovered the
Mississippi River. As one of Radisson's biographers says: "This
was undoubtedly the first time the upper Mississippi River
had been seen by white men, and its discovery may be
regarded as the outstanding accomplishment of these two
Frenchmen on their Mississippi voyage." We shall let M.
Radisson tell in his own words of this part of their voyage:

> We were four months in our voyage, without doing anything
> but go from river to river. We met several sorts of people. We
> conversed with them, being long time in alliance with them.
> By the persuasion of some of them we went into the great
> river that divides itself in two [believed to be the confluence
> of the Mississippi and Missouri] where the Hurons, with
> some Ottawa and the wildmen that had wars with them,
> had retired. There is no great difference in their language, as
> we were told. This nation have wars against those of [the]
> forked river [this may also refer to the Mississippi and/or
> Missouri]; it is so called because it has two branches, the one
> towards the west, the other towards the south, which we
> believe runs towards Mexico by the tokens they gave us. . . .

Radisson then devotes his attention briefly to the branch
running "towards the west," as follows:

> We were informed of that nation that live in the other river
> [i.e., the branch running toward the west—the Missouri].
> They were men of an extraordinary height and bigness.
> That made us believe they had no communication with
> them. They live only upon corn and citruls [pumpkins]
> which are mighty big. They have fish in plenty throughout
> the year. . . . Their dishes are made of wood. . . . They have
> great calumets [peace pipes] of great stones, red and green.
> They made a store of tobacco. They have a kind of drink

that makes them mad for a whole day.

As students of the Midwestern Indians know, the one tribe of Indians within the entire midlands area "of an extraordinary height and bigness" were the Osages, and they had by this time taken up residence in the lower Missouri. (Fort Osage, erected near today's Kansas City, was named after them.) Thus, it appears fairly clear that Radisson was writing, at this early date, about the Missouri.

The next historical reference to the Missouri-Mississippi river system was made by Père Marquette. It is not surprising that Marquette had information concerning the Missouri and Mississippi. As we have seen, the Ottawas, to whom he was missionary, for a long time had been making hunting trips as far west as the Rockies, from which areas they frequently brought back prisoners. It was thus only a matter of time before the full picture of the rivers to the west would become known to the French since Indian eyewitnesses were readily at hand. Most Kansas Citians would be surprised to learn how important a part their section of the country played in encouraging one of the epoch-making voyages of discovery in our history—the Marquette and Joliet expedition. Talon, the Intendant of New France, and Frontenac, the Governor-General, knew of the rumors of the great river (Mississippi) which ran from the lakes country southward, and they had reason to believe that it might lead them to the Gulf of California. But they had a bigger dream than merely to discover a river. Although the Europeans had discovered that a landmass intervened, their conception of it greatly foreshortened its east-west dimension, and they had still not given up Columbus' vision of an all-water route westward to the Orient. Frontenac's primary reason for sponsoring the expedition of Marquette and Joliet—as he himself stated—was to locate a water route to the west, past the province of Quivira in present south-central Kansas to the area of the fabled mines of New Mexico and thence to the China Sea (Pacific Ocean). As

Marquette's journal put it, the reasons were that:

> In the year 1673, Monsieur the Count de Frontenac, our
> Governor, and Monsieur Talon, then our intendant, recog-
> nizing the importance of this discovery—either that they
> might seek a passage from here to the sea of China, by the
> river that discharges into the Vermillion, or California Sea;
> or because they desired to verify what has for sometime been
> said concerning the two kingdoms of Theguaio and Quivira,
> which border on Canada, and in which numerous gold
> mines are reported to exist [sent an expedition, etc.].

This hoped-for route to the east by sailing west—and not
merely the Mississippi—was the lodestone of the voyage. As we
shall see, Marquette was convinced he had found this route
when he discovered the Missouri, and his fondest wish and
firm intention—cut short by his untimely death—was to be able
to explore the Missouri past our area and to its farthest reaches
in the hope that it would lead him to the China Sea. Probably
the next specific historical reference (after Nicolet's) to the
Missouri River occurs in Marquette's letter of 1670 to Father
Mercier, the Huron mission superior, wherein after a reference
to the Mississippi River, Marquette also added:

> Six or seven days journey below the Illinois [Indian villages]
> there is another great river on which live some very powerful
> nations, who use wooden canoes, of them we can write
> nothing else until next year—if God grant us the grace to
> conduct us thither.

The small party left Green Bay in May of 1673 and gained
the Mississippi via the Fox and Wisconsin rivers, toward the
end of June. In the late afternoon, shortly after passing some
Indian pictures of "monsters" near the site of present Alton,
Illinois, they came upon a phenomenon which brought the
existence of the vast Missouri River watershed to the west
violently to their—and history's—attention. We shall let Père
Marquette tell the story as an eyewitness:

While conversing about these monsters, sailing quietly in clear and calm water, we heard the noise of a rapid, into which we were about to run. I have seen nothing more dreadful. An accumulation of large and entire trees, branches, and floating islands were issuing from the mouth of the river pekistanoui, with such impetuosity that we could not without great danger risk passing through it. So great was the agitation that the water was very muddy and could not become clear.

The water was so muddy, indeed, that the Indian name *Peki(s)tanoui*, which Marquette thus applied to the Missouri River, meant "muddy water." Thus, the popular term "Big Muddy" has an ancient aboriginal lineage. Marquette then related his cherished hope and also revealed for the first time a great deal of new Midwestern geography, in the following passage:

Pekitanoui is a river of considerable size, coming from the northwest, from a great distance; and it discharges into the Mississippi. There are many villages of savages along this river, and I hope by its means to discover the Vermillion or California Sea. Judging from the direction of the course of the Mississippi, it discharges into the Mexican Gulf. . . . It would be a great advantage to find the river leading to the southern sea, toward California; and, as I have said, this is what I hope to do by means of the Pekitanoui, according to the reports made to me by the savages. From them I have learned that, by ascending this river for 5 or 6 days, one reaches a fine prairie, 20 or 30 leagues long. This must be crossed in a northwesterly direction, and it terminates at another small river,—on which one may embark, for it is not very difficult to transport canoes through so fine a country as that prairie. This second river flows toward the southwest for 10 or 15 leagues, after which it enters a lake, small and deep, which flows toward the west, where it falls into the sea. I have hardly any doubt that it is the Vermillion [California] Sea, and I do not despair of discovering it some day, if God grant me the grace and the health to do so, in order that I may preach The Gospel to all the peoples of this new world.

Allowing for errors in distance, this was a reasonably accurate description (obtained from the Indians) of the Missouri and western river systems which figure considerably in later history. It was also probably the first written account which necessarily traversed the Kansas City area. For the "5 or 6 days" trip by canoe up the Pekitanoui after which one reached "a fine prairie" which one "crossed in a northwesterly direction" would have taken one to the beginning of the prairies at the northerly bend of the Missouri River at present Kansas City. (If one started northwesterly sooner, one would later have to recross the Missouri—an important event which would have been mentioned in the narrative and a waste of effort since it was possible to have continued to that point via the easier water route.)

Not only did the Marquette-Joliet expedition result in our first written reference to include the Kansas City area, but it also gave us the first known maps of our area. One of them, Joliet's map of 1674, is beautifully reproduced in the *Jesuit Relations*. Although it fails to show the northerly bend of the Pekitanoui (and omits its name), it does give a decided northwesterly orientation to the river and correctly shows each of the Indian tribes in their then approximate distribution along the river: i.e., Missouri, Kansa, Ouchage (Osage), Pani (Pawnee), etc. Thus, on this rather ancient map of 1674 we see already the principal features of our area—the river running through the area and heading north and west, the vast prairie land on either side of the river, and the names Missouri and Kansa(s) in their proper east-west juxtaposition.

Marquette's map of 1673-74, although not drawn with as much skill, shows not only the river winding northwesterly, but also names it "Pekittanoui" and in addition shows the Indian tribes with the Osage downstream from the Missouri (a more current position). The river is not carried upstream past the Missouri and Kansa villages as in the Joliet map, however.

Père Marquette died in 1675 after making a second voyage down the Mississippi to establish a mission among the Kaskaskia Indians in the Illinois region. In view of his strongly expressed hope and purpose of exploring the Missouri, we can assume that he intended to and would have used the Kaskaskia mission as his advance base for such exploration, had he lived (just as St. Ignace in present Michigan served for his Mississippi trips). It seems a fitting tribute (among many) to his memory that Kansas Citians should realize the part which their river and their area played in the fondest hopes and aspirations of this brave and devout priest.

In 1682 Robert Cavelier de La Salle, also with Governor Frontenac's blessing, bettered the feat of Marquette and Joliet by descending the Mississippi all the way to the gulf. With him were twenty-three Frenchmen and thirty-one Indians. Traveling in the dead of winter, his party went through the Straits of Mackinac, down Lake Michigan's east coast, and around January 1, 1682 up the Chicago River (manhandling their canoes over solid ice) and down the Illinois. On February 6 of that year they came to the Mississippi (which they called the Colbert) but could not proceed for about a week because of ice in that river.

La Salle's faithful lieutenant, Henri de Tonty, added to the then knowledge of the Missouri country when he wrote the following (after returning to Quebec, in November, 1684):

. . . we descended the river, and found, at six leagues, upon the right hand, a river which fell into the River Colbert, which came from the west, and appeared to be as large and as considerable as the great river, according to the reports of the Indians. It is called the Emissourita [Missouri] and is well peopled. There are even villages of Indians which use horses to go to war and to carry the carcasses of the cattle [buffalo] which they kill.

Thus, we see added to the growing picture of the future Kansas City area and its hinterlands the name by which its river has been known ever since (Missouri) and a description of the plains Indians who dwelt hereabout and of the Spanish ponies they rode to make war and to hunt buffalo. Tonty wrote further concerning the Missouri when he made his rescue mission to aid the remnants of La Salle's second expedition. He stated that:

> The rivers of the Missouri came from the west, and, after traversing 300 leagues, arrive at a lake, which I believe to be that of the Apaches.

He also stated that on the voyage downriver, when they came to the Missouri, "we slept at its mouth." Still more details were filled in by Father Zenobius Membrè, a member of the expedition, who wrote:

> . . . and six leagues lower down we found the river of the Ozages [i.e., the Missouri on which resided the powerful tribe whose name is here used] coming from the west. It is full as large as the River Colbert, into which it empties, and which is so disturbed by it that from the mouth of this river the water is hardly drinkable. The Indians assured us that this river is formed by many others, and that they ascend it for ten or twelve days to a mountain where they have their source; and that beyond this mountain is the sea, where great ships are seen; that it is peopled by a great number of large villages, of several different nations; that there are lands and prairies, and great cattle and beaver hunting.

Here we have the first suggestion of the mountain systems which intervened between the Missouri Valley and the Pacific Ocean on which the "great ships" of the Spanish were seen. Also, the first statement that "many other" rivers (such as the Kansas) entered the Missouri. And, perhaps most important of all for the future development of our area, there is the first written mention of the great abundance of beaver. As we shall see, the European fancy for beaver hats and other items of apparel first titillated by Louis XIV, coupled with the prolific abundance and high quality of beaver pelts in the lands of the Osage and Kansa, brought a rush of commercial enterprise to our area. Beaver skins became of such importance as an article of commerce that they became legal tender and so easily ascertainable in value that in 1751 a promissory note was written at a post within the present metropolitan Kansas City area payable in beaver skins at the prevailing market at that post!

Nicholas de La Salle, also a member of the La Salle expedition, wrote in 1685:

> Finally we descended the Mississippi. The first day we camped six leagues on the right bank, near the mouth of a river which falls into the Mississippi and is very impetuous and muddy. It is named the river of the Missouris. The river comes from the northwest. It is well peopled, according to what the Indians say. The Panis [Pawnees] are upon this river, a great distance from its mouth.

A most important result of La Salle's expedition, for purposes of our inquiry, is the fact that upon reaching the mouth of the Mississippi on April 9, 1682, he claimed it and all lands drained by it and its tributaries for France, thus making the present Kansas City area (and all of Louisiana) a part of the domains of Louis XIV.

In 1684 La Salle carried out an ambitious, but poorly planned, colonizing expedition to Louisiana by sailing directly from France to the gulf. La Salle was unable to locate the mouth of the Mississippi, the colony was a disastrous failure, and La Salle was himself murdered by his own men. One of the survivors of this expedition who with a small party of companions made his way north up the Mississippi (which they found belatedly) was Fr. Anastasius Douay, a priest. The party passed the mouth of the Missouri in 1687, and concerning it Father Douay wrote:

About six leagues below this mouth [of the Illinois River] there is on the northwest the famous river of the Massourites, or Ozages, at least as large as the main river into which it empties; it is formed by a number of other known rivers everywhere navigable and inhabited by many populous tribes. They include also the Ozages, who have seventeen villages on a river of their name which empties into that of the Massourites, to which the maps have also extended the name of Ozages.

Thus, as early as 1687, we are given the rather remarkable information that the Missouri is "famous," that the main tributary systems of the Missouri (Osage, Grand, Kansas, Platte, etc.) were not only "known" (presumably by the Indians, who told the French) but also were known to be navigable, and that the maps—just whose maps we are not told—showed the Osage River and so named it. Perhaps these maps even showed the Kansas River at the bend of the Missouri, since it was the next large navigable tributary upstream from the Osage, and the Kansa tribe who dwelt in its area were by 1687 fairly well known to the French.

Up to this point, we have been looking at the Midwest through Indian eyes, so to speak, since the accounts of the French were virtually all gained secondhand from the savages who traded with the French. Now we shall consider the celebrated (or perhaps notorious is more fitting) account of one who claimed to have gone up the Missouri to see for himself. This account was entitled "New Voyages to North-America" by its author, Baron Louis-Armand Lahontan et Hesleche—commonly referred to as Lahontan. His father was a highly competent civil engineer who had been given a pension and a monopoly on the commerce at the harbor of Bayonne by Louis XIV in return for valuable services. The family fortunes were at a low ebb when Louis reached young manhood, however, and he went to Canada as an officer in the Bourbon regiment. After serving there for a time, he was assigned to the post of commandant at Fort St. Joseph in 1687. Due to reports from the east of degeneration of the French position there, he determined to abandon his wilderness position and return to the French settlements, and set out to do so on August 27, 1688, arriving at Fort Michilimakinac in the late summer. He determined to return to Montreal via the southern route instead of wintering at the fort. It was while on this extended trip that he made his supposed journey up the Missouri. On the seventeenth of March, 1689, Lahontan's party, while descending the Mississippi, arrived at the mouth of the Missouri. Lahontan wrote:

> . . . in four days time, by the help of the current and our oars, (we) made the River of the Missouris. This done, we run up against the stream of that river which was at least as rapid as the Mississippi was at that time; and arrived on the 18th at the first village of the Missouris, where I only stopped to make the people some presents that procured me a hundred turkeys, with which that people are wonderfully well stocked. After that, we rowed hard against the stream, and landed next night near the second Village. [Next followed an altercation resulting in a hasty departure by the French.] To be short, we re-embarked that same day, about two o'clock in the afternoon, and rowed about four leagues up the River, where we made the River of the Osages, and encamped by its mouth. That night we had several false alarms from the wild Beeves [buffalo] upon which we made sufficient reprisals afterwards; for the next day we killed many of them.

Another encounter with the savages cut short their stay on the Missouri, and Lahontan and his men returned downriver to the Mississippi, reaching it on March 25, 1689. Lahontan included in his book, published in 1703, two maps which portray not only the Missouri and the Osage rivers, but also extend the Missouri River in a northwesterly direction which, if one could trust his scale (which is uncertain), would include

the Kansas City area. Certainly he was the nearest observer up
to his time. One wonders why the Kansa were not mentioned
(as Marquette had), but perhaps at this early date they had
not attained a sufficiently definite differentiation of identity
from the parent Siouan stock and were still considered
"Missouris" or "Osages" by many.

So much for what Lahontan may in fact have done on the
Missouri. We cannot leave him, however, without referring to
another claimed voyage of his which he could not possibly
have taken—since it is about 95 percent apocryphal. What
interests us in this fictitious voyage up the "Long River,"
however, is not the bit of hokum which the baron perpetrated
upon his readers, but the rather startling five percent (to pick a
figure) of amazingly accurate geographical fact upon which he
hangs his tale. His biographer, Thwaites, said that the story
seemed to be made up of bits he had possibly garnered from
the Indians, Father Membrè, La Salle, Père Marquette, and
Hennepin. He simply didn't realize that he should have added
his description of the "Long River" to the end of his Missouri
journey. He got off to a good start when he said that the
Panimohas (Pawnees) lived upstream and were enemies of the
local Indians. But when he described it as the "least rapid river
in the world" where "great calm always prevails" and which
was "clean and free from rocks and beds of sand" and yet went
all the way to the mountains, no one who knew the actual facts
could fail to hold such dissembling against him.

In any event, however he got the information and whether
he was ever there or not, he tells that there were trees on hills
along the banks at first, with meadows stretching away here
and there; later on there was open country and the land
became so barren there was not even a chip of wood for a fire;
there was ice in several places, frozen hard (it was then
December, 1689); and 80 leagues southward were Indians who
were "well acquainted with the Spaniards of New Mexico."
The Spaniards themselves were not over 240 leagues away (in
a southerly direction.) Lahontan then gives a convincing

description of the Rocky Mountains:

> Their [his Indian host's] Villages stand upon a River that
> springs out of a ridge of Mountains from which the Long
> River likewise derives its source, there being a great many
> Brooks there which by a joint confluence form the River.
> The Mountains I spoke of but now are six leagues broad,
> and so high that one must cast an infinity of windings and
> turnings before he can cross them. Bears and wild beasts are
> their only inhabitants.

As if to confound us by larding his fiction with more
surprisingly accurate fact, he goes on to say:

> [The western Savages] informed me, that at the distance of
> 150 Leagues from the place where I then was, their principal
> river empties itself into a *Salt Lake* of three hundred leagues
> in circumference.

The remarkable thing about Lahontan's foregoing descriptions is that by ascending the Missouri and then the Platte, or
possibly the Cheyenne, one would have come to a place far out
on the great plains where, in December, it would indeed have
been barren with hardly a chip of wood for a fire, where the
river would have been frozen solid with ice, where early tribes
of Plains Indians lived who traded with the Spaniards to the
south, and which was adjacent to the Rockies which indeed
were high, wide, tortuous to traverse and the home of bears
and other animals, and beyond which lay unique Great *Salt*
Lake, largest salt lake in North America and nearly "three
hundred leagues in circumference." This was more than
imagination!

Lahontan supplied a map as well, on which he not only
displayed all of the above features and included a very realistic
chain of mountains wending north and south in the approximate position of the Rockies, but also capped this off with
another great river system flowing *west*! Whatever we may
think of Lahontan's misrepresentation of some of the facts, we

must give him his due as a reporter. Others before him had made passing reference to the features of the West. He, however, was the first to put the pieces of Kansas City's western hinterland into one composite whole—the Long River (essentially the Missouri and its upstream tributaries), the Great Plains and the Indians who lived there, the turkeys, buffalos and bears, the Spaniards to the southwest, the great Continental Divide formed by the Rocky Mountains, Great Salt Lake, and the rivers of the Pacific Northwest.

The wish is father to the act. What may have been fantasy for Lahontan become solid fact not long thereafter. In 1699 the Jesuits established a mission at Cahokia in the Illinois country (now a suburb of East St. Louis) and a settlement grew up near the mission. This settlement became in turn an advance base (as Père Marquette had no doubt envisaged) for travel up the Missouri. Did Frenchmen actually visit the future site of Kansas City before the end of the 1600s? The best that one can say is that the chances are exceedingly good that a number of them did so during the last two decades of that century, as will be seen below. To place this period in historical context, the year 1688, for example, was only a century after the defeat of the Spanish Armada, was the year in which Louis XIV was putting the finishing touches on his palace at Versailles, and was a century before ratification of the U. S. Constitution.

The revolt of the pueblos at Taos in 1680, although 600 miles from Kawsmouth, nevertheless had a profound effect on western history. Just at the time the Spanish were scurrying for El Paso (not to return for nearly 20 years), the French were starting to penetrate the Mississippi and its tributaries in great numbers—filling the trading void left by the Spanish in the high plains, Colorado, and New Mexico. It did not take the French long to discover Taos and its annual trade fair, and, of course, Santa Fe.

As early as 1680 or 1681 two Frenchmen had taken up residence, perforce, with some of the Missouri tribe, for La Salle spoke of them in his writings. They had been captured by the Missouris on the Mississippi and taken by them to their own village upstream on the Missouri.

In May and June of 1693, two other French traders, in company with some Kaskaskia Indians, went up the river as far as the Osage and Missouri villages. Their purpose was to open trading relations between these tribes and the French at the Illinois. This information was reported in a letter of Father Gravier's dated 1694.

In 1695 an Indian chief stated that he had heard a rumor that Henri de Tonty (La Salle's lieutenant who later served at the Arkansas and Illinois posts) had been directed by French Governor Frontenac in Canada to "go to war against the Kanzas." This, incidentally, is apparently the first historical reference to the Kanza in other than purely geographical terms.

Father St. Cosme made a visit to the Missouri area in 1698 and made a firsthand report on the Indians in this region. He gives no indication of having reached the Kaw, however.

The Osage were the strongest nation on the lower Missouri River, and once the French had established friendly relations with them (as they did in 1693) and learned their language, they would have a ready entrée to the Kansa. The Kansa no doubt heard at an early date from their Siouan cousins, the Osage, of the wonders which the French had to trade in return for mere beaver skins.

A serious blow was dealt to French expansionist activities in the West in 1696. As early as 1666 Colbert had urged in a letter to Canadian Intendant Talon that it would be wise "to restrict oneself to an expanse of country that the colony itself could maintain, rather than to grasp too vast an area and perhaps one day be obliged to abandon part of it." The Montreal and Quebec merchants were vociferously in support of such a policy, for somewhat more limited personal reasons, since they wanted beaver furs to be traded at their stores, rather than in the hinterland. As a result, for a number of years prior to 1696, trading in the West had been limited to twenty-five licensees per year. Those in favor of restricting the western expansion finally won out completely in 1696 when Louis XIV and his Minister, Pontchartrain, decided to make virtually a complete withdrawal from the West. All *congé* licenses were revoked and the traders were ordered to return with their merchandise to the eastern posts. All military and trading posts in the West were closed except four, and trading was strictly forbidden at such posts. But this fiat was short-lived. For soon after New Orleans was founded, and it was realized that Mississippi valley posts could supply it with trade and provide stability among the Indians and a bulwark against the encroaching English. The court—far too late—did a complete about-face and in 1700 and 1701 began to encourage the western trade again. Thus, "no longer were coureurs de bois regarded as renegades and outlaws; whether they realized it or not they had suddenly been transmuted into agents of French imperialism." After 1700, the floodgates of trade up the Missouri were opened wide.

One gets the impression from the meager French records of the period that the French had ascended a considerable distance up the Missouri beyond present Kansas City even by 1700. In Penicaut's *Annals of Louisiana,* the author speaking of his own trip to the upper Mississippi with Le Sueur in 1700, says (July 12):

> We ascended the Mississippi six leagues higher, where we found, on the left, the mouth of a very large river named the Missoury. Up to the present the source of the Missoury has not been found, nor that of the Mississippy. I will not speak of the manners of the inhabitants of the banks of the Missoury, because I have not yet ascended the Missoury.

This seems to imply that *some* Frenchmen had sought the source of the Missouri, and that the writer considered it a fairly routine trip which he himself simply hadn't had occasion to undertake as yet.

Fr. James Gravier, a Jesuit missionary, wrote in 1700 about

his trip down the Mississippi. Speaking of the Arkansas River, he noted that it ran to the northwest, and that "by ascending it, one reaches the river of the Missouris, by making a portage." Since one wouldn't be likely to portage across the Ozark (French, *aux arcs*) Mountains, he was presumably referring to actual French trips to the flatlands commencing at about the present eastern border of Kansas.

From the turn of the century on there were in almost every year one or more reports of expeditions up the Missouri to the Kaw and beyond, and these reports were frequently accompanied by maps. In March of 1702, according to Father Bergier, seventeen Frenchmen left the Tamoroa village in the Illinois region and ascended the Missouri with the intention of building a fort in the Pawnee country. They were turned back somewhere en route by an Indian attack, however.

On February 15, 1703, twenty French-Canadians left the same Tamoroa village bound for New Mexico to trade and investigate the mines (they too were turned back en route by the Indians). Colbert had said as early as 1669 that the French were "looking for mines everywhere," and after the renewal of the western trade this policy was pursued in western America with vigor. Chevalier Pierre Charles Le Sueur, a famous mining engineer, reported that on one of his trips up the Mississippi (in 1703) he encountered an entrepreneur who "a little time later went with twenty young men to the Kansas." Perhaps this was the same group which left February 15 of the same year. We have no further report on their activities. By 1704 there were about 110 Frenchmen working the Missouri fur trade in groups of seven or eight. While on the return leg of a mining expedition to the upper Mississippi, Le Sueur is said to have ascended the Missouri as far as the Kaw. If he left a journal of this trip, it has not come to light. While the records are not altogether clear, engineer Le Sueur's testimony is certainly more probative than adventurer Lahontan's, and he is in any event the first non-Indian said to have viewed the present site of Kansas City whose name we definitely know.

His title of "Chevalier," incidentally, indicated that he had
been awarded by Louis XIV the royal and military order of
the Cross of St. Louis (XI), no mean accomplishment in that
day. Thus may Kansas City's actual history really be said to
have commenced almost three centuries ago. Perhaps Kansas
City should remember the name of the Chevalier Pierre
Charles Le Sueur.

Another facet of French trade up the Missouri bears
mention here. Taos and its annual Taos Fair figured rather
prominently in the minds of individual French traders on the
Missouri, and in the French and Spanish literature of the
period, during much of the very late 1600s and early 1700s.
There was almost a "tale of two cities" aspect to the relationship between Kawsmouth, the *chef lieu* of the Missouri
River traders, and Taos—the nearest point of European
civilization to the west. Taos Pueblo, with its multi-story
"skyscraper" aspect, still held a golden fascination for the
French, akin to the old "Seven Cities of Cíbola" myths of the
Spanish. The Taos Indians seem to have been living at their
pueblo on the mesa east of the Rio Grande gorge in front of
their beloved mountain with their cold rushing stream, pan-
oramic view, and pungent pinon fires for around *500 years before
1700!* They were engaged in large-scale trading operations
even during the early Spanish period, as attested by two
reports of 1561 and 1630. Coronado's lieutenant, Castenada,
wrote in 1561 (referring to their portable bazaar carried on
trains of pack dogs) that "They go trading like Arabs."
Another Spaniard wrote in 1630 that "thus the people carry
their merchandise laden, which they barter for cotton cloth
and other things they need."

When the Taos Indians rose in revolt against the Spanish in
1680, *every Spaniard* was driven from the entire present state of
New Mexico (or killed), leaving these avid traders and
consumers of European goods at Taos with no source of
supply. Enter the French. They were literally catapulted into
the trade vacuum thus created (although uninvited), and

many of them lost their scalps in the process. For, to make matters more interesting, the fierce Comanches, inveterate raiders and incomparable horsemen, moved down into the plains east of Taos at about the same time. There is a valuable source of information available on this French westward expansion from other than French reports. Naturally, the French coureurs de bois (whose activities were still frowned upon by Frontenac) did not publicize their activities in the hinterland. But the Spanish authorities in the Southwest, whose theoretical authority extended to the Missouri River and beyond, dutifully reported in detail on every shred of information on French penetration in their direction. Several times the Spanish authorities were surprised to learn that individual Frenchmen had attended the Taos Fair, but their visits were brief and none of them were apprehended. In 1694 some white (and apparently French) children were captured on the plains northeast of New Mexico by the Navahos and beheaded when the Spanish would not ransom them. In 1695, the Apaches reported to the New Mexican authorities that "a large number of French are coming towards the plains of Cíbola." Similar reports were received in 1697, 1698, and 1699 in each of which years there were celebrated encounters between the French and Pawnees on the one hand and the Spanish-supported Navahos. These were on occasion authenticated with French trade goods and other paraphernalia. One Navaho raid on the Pawnees (in 1698) netted the participants a collection of French jewels, carbines, cannons, powder flasks, gamellas, sword belts, waistcoats, shoes, and small brass pots. Since the Pawnees were located northward through Kansas and perhaps southern Nebraska at this time, these Frenchmen must have come up the Missouri past Kawsmouth and the site of present-day Kansas City.

By 1700, the Spanish had begun to reestablish their control over Taos, the northernmost pueblo outpost of their Mexican empire. The stage was set for the heyday of the annual Taos Fairs. These were the fairs which A. B. Thomas, writing of a period as early as 1715, described as "the periodic fairs held in the ... pueblos." The Comanches eventually became the mainstay of the Taos Fairs (although not formally welcome until about 1748), and one writer even referred to "the Comanche fair at Taos." They plundered the Comancheria, an area about 400 miles wide and 600 miles north and south, sparsely settled by Spanish, Mexicans, and Indians (and eventually the French and Anglos). The spoils they brought to the Taos Fair. In 1744 (the year Fort Cavagnial was founded) a Spanish priest described the Taos Fair thus:

> This Mission ... is the first one to which most of the tribes come together for their fairs which are governed by the moon and which the Governor (of New Mexico) and his Lieutenant Governor attend with many neighbors and soldiers.

It was said that people came from as far away as Guadalajara to attend the Taos Fair! But this is not too surprising when we realize that the French traders traveled nearly an equal distance from the Illinois country past Kawsmouth and across the plains to get to the Fair. Bishop Tamaron, on a pastoral call in 1760, described the Taos Fair as follows:

> The Comanches remained on the Los Animas River hunting buffalo, in order to come to the [Taos] fairs; every year they come to the fairs. The Governor [of New Mexico] comes with a great part of his presidio and people from all over the Kingdom to these fairs, which they call ransoms. They [Comanches] bring captives to sell, buckskins, many buffalo hides and booty that they have taken in other parts—horses, guns, muskets, ammunition, knives, meat and various other things. No money circulates in these fairs but articles are traded for each other and in this way these people [the Taosenos] provide for themselves.

The bishop said there were 70 Comanche tents pitched at this fair (around 700 people) which with several thousand

Taos Indians and Spaniards and Frenchmen must have been quite a gathering! There would hardly have been room for the Comanche tents on the pueblo plaza, and they must have made their camp out on the mesa.

Daniel J. Weber in his book, *The Taos Trappers*, describes the later Taos Fair as follows:

> During the last half of the eighteenth century the [Taos] valley became the scene of New Mexico's most important trade fair. Usually during July or August Spanish settlers, government officials, and Pueblos from throughout the province would gather at Taos to trade with neighboring tribes—unless they were at war with them that year. . . . Years of trading with neighboring tribes served to give the Taos Valley a "cosmopolitan" flavor which . . . trappers would find attractive and useful. By 1776, the Taosenos already were reputed to speak the languages of the Utes, Apaches, Comanches and Pueblos [plus Spanish and French]. Thus, mountain men would find translators at Taos, some of whom could also serve as excellent guides.

The Comanches usually raised considerable hell on the way to and from the Taos Fair, raiding Spanish and Indian settlements. Some years they would be trading at one pueblo while raiding and killing at another one a few miles away at the same time. In 1760 they attacked Taos itself, killing all the fighting men and carrying off 50 women, and the next year they returned to the fair as if nothing had happened. This was too much for the Spanish, who barred them from the fair until the next year, when the contrite Comanches signed a peace treaty.

What does all this have to do with Kansas City and the French? The Taos-Santa Fe trade drew them like a magnet in the intervals between Franco-Spanish wars and Comanche war parties. They heard rumors of the fair and had visions of making fabulous profits exchanging trade goods for Spanish silver—perhaps even gold! It must be admitted that the

presence of dark-eyed señoritas was also a lure. The French
coureurs de bois drifted across the plains in twos and threes,
according to reports which, while terse, are literally too
numerous to quote here. These were the "woods rangers"—the
drifters—who pre-dated the more institutionalized commercial
system of *fermiers*, *voyageurs*, and *engagés* which came later. The
trade eventually grew so brisk and French interest so high that
Bourgmont risked his life getting the Comanche treaty for the
French Crown in 1724 in order to open up the Taos-Santa Fe
trade route. Taos and its fair were, in effect, the first south-
western terminus of what was eventually to become the Santa
Fe Trail out of Kansas City. The importance to French Kansas
City history of these developments is that they added just that
much more impetus to French military and trade expansion
up the Missouri River and in the vicinity of Kawsmouth
during the already rapid expansion occurring throughout the
early and middle 1700s.

While these feeble French penetrations were being carried
out up the Missouri, momentous things were happening to the
embattled Bourbon regime in continental Europe. As Marcel
Wallenstein, for years the European correspondent for the
Kansas City *Star*, has succinctly noted:

> The sun of France began to set with the battles of Blenheim
> (1704), Ramilles (1706) and Malplaquet (1709.) The power
> of the French tyrant (Louis XIV) was broken by the genius
> of Marlborough (Churchill's ancestor) and Eugene (Prince
> of Savoy.) But for these three men, who lived at the end of
> the 17th and into the early 18th century, there might be
> open air cafes along the Missouri River, grapes planted on
> the hills of Jackson and Buchanan Counties. Courts would
> be administered according to the French code instead of the
> English common law. And the whole civilization of our
> beautiful Missouri valley would be colored by French
> instead of Anglo-Saxon tradition.

CHAPTER II

De Bourgmont and Fort Orleans

THE MOST IMPORTANT—and by far the most colorful—personage to visit the Kansas City area during the French colonial period was Etienne Veniard, Sieur de Bourgmont. His fascinating life reads like fiction, and it is surprising no one has written his biography. He was born in France in about 1680, the son of Charles de Veniard, Sieur de Vergie, a physician of Normandy. He was said to be a "giant of a man," a descendant of the Norman Vikings. He was the nephew of the Vicar General of the powerful Bishop of Quebec, a fact which may explain why he always seemed to be given the benefit of the doubt during several periods of official disfavor. Young Etienne eschewed a comfortable life in France to enlist in the military and endure the rigors of the American wilds. No likeness of him appears to be extant, and we must content ourselves with the romanticized versions appearing in the Missouri Valley Room of the Kansas City Public Library and on the east frieze of the City Hall.

He was an officer in the garrison at Quebec during the governorship of the celebrated Frontenac. If he was not overtly enlisted, like Marquette, La Salle, Tonty, Nicolet, and Cadillac, as one of Frontenac's "disciples" to open up the West (as one is certainly tempted to surmise), he must at least have learned from the governor or those close to him of the intriguing lands drained by the Mississippi and the Missouri. He got an early initiation into the fur trade in 1702, at which time he built a fort and set up a tannery for St. Denis (Lt.

General at Three Rivers) at the confluence of the Ohio and Mississippi. He then spent 18 months among the Mascoutins procuring pelts for the venture (which proved unsuccessful). He participated in the defense of Detroit against the Fox Indians in 1712, having succeeded Alphonse de Tonty as commandant of that post in January, 1706.

It was while he was stationed at Detroit that Bourgmont made a chance acquaintance which was to change the course of his life and which eventually brought him to the Missouri country. One of the tribes which rallied to the aid of the French in defending the Detroit post against the Fox Indians was that of the Missouris. This tribe so impressed him—and he them—that an unshakable bond of friendship grew up between them. As we shall see, this friendship was to stand Bourgmont in good stead in later years.

Shortly after the Fox raid, an untoward event took place involving Bourgmont, the details of which are obscure. One version has it that he absconded with an officer's wife (some say Cadillac's wife, others Madame Tichenet) and went to live in the woods as a coureur de bois. This version is the most implausible, since Cadillac eventually personally helped to restore him to official favor, and neither of the ladies implicated were the sort one would expect to relish a life *au sauvage*. Another has it that Bourgmont alienated an important Kansa chief, and through him the chiefs of the other tribal allies, by upbraiding the chief severely when he beat Bourgmont's dog. Still a third story—and one which is actually borne out by later events (including the very tangible evidence of the birth of a son)—is that he became enamoured of a beautiful Missouri Indian maid and eloped with her. As early as 1708 he was reported to be sharing his life with an Indian woman. Bourgmont clearly had a son by his Missouri common-law wife, for he said on a later trip (in 1724) that the boy accompanied him, apparently on horseback.

In any event, through one or a combination of the above causes, Bourgmont abandoned (or was relieved of his duties at) his post at Detroit and went to live with the Missouri Indians when they returned to their home country in 1713 after the Fox campaign. Their villages at that time were on the Missouri across from the mouth of the Grand River. We have seen previously that French traders had, since about 1680, been in residence with the Missouris. Like all of the coureurs de bois they ignored official laws and regulations. The Jesuit fathers at Kaskaskia, in 1713, despaired of the "Scandalous and Criminal life" of these woods rangers on the Missouri, including Bourgmont.

In 1713, Bourgmont set out on a remarkable survey of the Missouri River as far as the Platte. He actually started his report at the mouth of the Mississippi, but it is best known for its wealth of detail on the then relatively undescribed Missouri. This amazingly thorough report must have been intended for the use of either the French military forces, or for the Company of the West (which not long thereafter published this report and commissioned Bourgmont a captain in its service). Bourgmont himself knew the route well, and his Indian associates had no need for an elaborate written French report on their own river. Probably Pontchartrain, Louis XIV's Minister of Finance, had ordered the report in furtherance of the empire's plans for the exploitation of Louisiana. As previously noted, the conclusion is almost inescapable that Bourgmont was in some way acting as agent for Louis XIV's governmental interest. Whatever the reason, Bourgmont prepared a running narrative of the physical characteristics of the route which read almost like a riverboat pilot's log. He noted distances down to a quarter of a league, described prominent hills, islands, prairies, and intersecting rivers and streams and added comments concerning the trees and other cover encountered. As literature it is deadly dull, and Baron Villiers has said rightly that in its entirety it possesses only three or four words which could be called colorful. Nevertheless it is the first on-the-spot description of our area (and of the entire Missouri River region to the Platte) and as such holds considerable

interest for us. The particular part of the journal of most
interest to us is the entry for Friday the eleventh of July, 1713,
which reads as follows:

> Friday the 11th—towards the southwest 3 q. of a league—
> towards the west Half a league—during the half league on
> the west side a range of hills—towards the west northwest a
> q. of a league, afterwards one finds the River of the Canzes,
> which mouth comes from the south—about a quarter of a
> league up this river (Canzes) and east of it, one sees crusts of
> Red Earth and a q. of a league higher up one sees a large
> island.

Taken in the context of the rest of the journal, this short note
reveals quite a bit of information. First, it is apparent from the
daily entries that Bourgmont did not travel at night—as was
usual in those days of the pirogue and canoe. Also, his average
day's travel at this point of the trip was nearly three and
one-half leagues. Since he only made a league and one-half on
this date, he probably sojourned for at least half a day in the
Kansas City area—perhaps going up the Kansas a short
distance to investigate the "Red Earth." (This may have been
the brick clay from which the Kansas City French later made
their chimneys.) His overnight stop on the tenth would have
been about where the Chouteau Bridge is now located (though
on which side we have no way of knowing). Three-fourths of a
league to the southwest would have taken him to approximately the present location of the Paseo Bridge. In the next
half league Bourgmont floated past the "range of hills" on the
"west" (actually south) side upon which present downtown
Kansas City is now situated. If the future potential of the site
made any impression upon him, he kept his thoughts to
himself. The then existing meandering pattern of the river
must have taken it past the present downtown area at a
location further north than now exists. For if we superimpose
Bourgmont's directions and distances upon the available space
between the bluffs, we see that the last three-quarters of a

league (up to the mouth of the Kansas) necessarily took him right across what is now the center of the landing field of the old Kansas City Municipal Airport! Somewhere in that general area was the mouth of the Kansas River. There he moored his craft, perhaps did some local exploring or treated with the Kansa Indians, and eventually spent the night of July 11, 1713—the first definitely known overnight visitor to the Kansas City area. Due to changes in the channel of the Kaw, it is impossible to say what composed the "Red Earth" Bourgmont saw east of that river, nor does anything remain of his "large island." The next day he made two and three-quarters leagues, and probably spent the night somewhere in the vicinity of Parkville, Missouri. From there, league by league, he traced his course up the Missouri as far as the Arickara Indian villages beyond the Platte.

Bourgmont apparently wrote up the journal of his voyage during the next year, 1714. It was published in France a few years later, during the Regency. His efforts were appreciated, for on September 25, 1718, Governor Bienville (the founder of New Orleans) requested the Council of the Regency to award him the Cross of St. Louis. He seems thereafter to have spent some time in the French military service in Louisiana. In May 1719, he participated in the French and Indian attack on, and capture of, Spanish Pensacola, in present Florida. Later in 1719 Governor Bienville of Louisiana petitioned that he be awarded a captain's commission as a reward for his services in exploring the Missouri and assisting in keeping the Indians under control. Interestingly enough, this commission was granted by the Company of the Indies (which then controlled Louisiana) and the original thereof, handwritten on parchment, is now in the archives of the Missouri Historical Society at St. Louis. Bienville sent Bourgmont to France late in 1719 for the purpose of reporting on his discoveries up the Mississippi and Missouri. On September 13, 1719, the Council of the Regency spoke highly of Bourgmont's services and determined to request that he be left in the Missouri area. But he was already en route to France so nothing came of this particular appointment.

We leave Bourgmont temporarily now to look at events in Europe which were to thrust him on a larger stage and result in his return to North America as the emissary of his country and his King to build a bridge of friendship from France to Spain in North America—starting at Fort Orleans. The history of Fort Orleans, to the east of present Kansas City near Brunswick, Missouri, was a microcosm of the Regency period—the era between Louis XIV's death and Louis XV's adulthood—which set the tone for the remainder of the Bourbon dynasty up to the Revolution. "Regency" furniture and decor and the paintings by Watteau of the idyllic *fetes galantes* are the hallmark of this era. Fort Orleans, indeed, was about as short-lived as the Regency itself.

To set the stage, we must look to events on the continent. France was insolvent when Louis XIV died, leaving as successor his five-year-old great-grandson Louis XV. And she was faced with an awkward internecine squabble between Louis XIV's profligate nephew, the Duc d'Orleans (a title somewhat, but not completely, equivalent to the Prince of Wales in the Bourbon dynasty) and Louis XIV's grandson, King Philip V of Spain. In his last illness, Louis told the assembled nobles "my nephew (Orleans) will govern the realm." Calling Orleans to his deathbed, Louis XIV said "You are about to see one king in his tomb and another in his cradle. Always cherish the memory of the first and the interests of the second." Orleans, as premier prince of the blood royal, found it necessary to defend his right to govern France as Regent in the so-called "War of the Spanish Succession" (1719-1720). Orleans was the victor, but the war engendered considerable financial anxiety and jockeying for position in Europe and the North American mainland by France and Spain. These twin problems, money and Spain, were the raison d'être for Fort Orleans.

On the monetary side, the Regent was desperate to solve the

problems bequeathed by his uncle. John Law's bizarre economic schemes appealed to the Regent as a means of recouping the state's fortunes after the military excesses of Louis XIV had all but drained the treasury. While the details need not concern us here, the central idea of the whole plan was predicated upon the material riches which were supposed to flow quickly and effortlessly to France from the Mississippi Company (whose territory included present Kansas City). Hence the name "Mississippi Bubble." Law even went so far as to display bars of gold in the windows of the company office in Paris. The company envisioned fabulous profits of silver and gold in exchange for its goods. Unfortunately, the bubble broke, Law fled to England and eventually Venice, and the Mississippi Company defaulted on its obligations and went bankrupt. But to keep the central government from going bankrupt along with its alter ego the company, a new enterprise, the Company of the Indies, was formed in 1719 to pick up the pieces and salvage whatever could be gleaned from the debacle. One of these assets to which the Company of the Indies succeeded was the right to trade for furs up the Missouri River.

A contributing factor, economically, was the longstanding French interest, extending from Champlain through Frontenac and later governors, in a water route to the western ocean and the supposed trade with the Spanish (and Chinese) which it was felt such a route would offer. Louisiana Governor Bienville had been lobbying for exploration of such a route for years, and his subordinate and second in command at the Illinois, Du Tisne, after a trip to the Pawnee country in 1719 (skirting beyond the southern reaches of the Kansas City metropolitan area) had made specific recommendations to the Company of the Indies that a fort be established on the Missouri River and that from it an expedition should be sent out to make peace with (and between) the plains tribes in order to open up trade with them as well as with the Spaniards in New Mexico. New Orleans (named after the Regent) was founded by Law's Company of the Indies in 1718 as an advance base for trade up the Mississippi.

Militarily, the situation in the western Louisiana area cried out for a French presence. Boisbriant, a commandant at the Illinois (and Governor Bienville's nephew), in 1719 joined in urging a post on the Missouri. Although peace had been declared between Spain and France earlier that year, it remained rather academic on the frontier. The Spanish in 1720 had sent a sizable armed expedition under Villasur to dislodge the French from the Pawnee country in southern Nebraska. A vicious battle ensued when the Spaniards (guided by the traitorous Frenchman L'Archeveque who had helped to murder La Salle) encountered the French-backed Pawnee somewhere along the Platte River on August 14, 1720. Bienville told the Council of the Regency in a dispatch dated April 25, 1722, that the Spanish, according to the Missouri Indians, were going to build a fort on the Kansas River and he had therefore ordered Boisbriant "to send a detachment of twenty soldiers to construct there a small fort and to keep a garrison there on the same river." This particular fort was never built, nor was its Spanish counterpart. But plans did proceed for a fort on the Missouri, and it is probable that the governor was really referring loosely to his knowledge that Bourgmont was about to depart upriver to establish Fort Orleans somewhere in the vicinity of Kawsmouth.

Hence it transpired in the early 1720s that both the Company of the Indies and the military almost simultaneously became acutely aware of the need for a competent individual to undertake the job of ascending the Mississippi and Missouri, establishing a fortified base of operations on the Missouri, and paving the way for amicable trade relations all the way across present Missouri, Kansas, Colorado, and New Mexico. The job was complicated by the fact that of the tribes to be brought into friendly alliance, several were at war with each other and two, the Pawnees and Comanches, had been considered prime sources for slaves by the Illinois tribes (and the French). Added to this was the fact that some of the French traders had been selling guns to various tribes and wanted to foster, rather than allay, their internecine strife.

Apparently the unanimous choice for this ambitious undertaking was none other than the erstwhile lawless woods ranger and soldier of fortune—Etienne Veniard, Sieur de Bourgmont. One can hardly escape the impression that from Louis XIV's last years on, Bourgmont was serving in a quasi-governmental status as a supplier of information and a serious student of his area and its tribes—biding his time and learning the language, like Nicolet, until his country needed to call upon his talents and friendly contacts. The clarion call went out in 1721. Perhaps not altogether by coincidence, Bourgmont was in France at the time, ready to accept the call.

The France (and particularly Paris) to which Bourgmont had returned was at the height of the Regency period—a free-thinking (and free-living) reaction to the staid and austere reign of Louis XIV and his pious Queen. The Regent, Orleans, himself set the pattern with his riotous life-style, his mistresses, and his roué friends. Fashionable parties were the rage, and they continued in endless succession, faithfully depicted by the painter Watteau, whose beautiful renditions of the *fetes galantes* are a mirror of the age. Fashionable salons presided over by some of France's most beautiful, intelligent, and well-dressed women were the order of the day, and the subjects were those of the Enlightenment—of Voltaire and others in the vanguard of liberal thought. Science was blossoming. Buffon, for example, was soon to begin assembling at his home and later at the Jardin des Plantes in Paris the flora and fauna of the world—indeed his correspondents included naturalists on the various expeditions up the Mississippi and Missouri, probably even to present Kansas City. But, as Bourgmont was to discover, the people who were best able to enjoy the good life of the Regency were the noblesse—to them all doors were open and a ready purse was available. But Bourgmont was a commoner. So he had a condition—modest enough in view of the feat he was to accomplish—upon which he insisted. If he successfully carried out the desires of the Court, the company, and the military by building his fort, making the great treaty, and bringing some Indian chiefs to Paris, then he wanted to be made a nobleman. Such upward mobility was another hallmark of the Regency period. His letter to the Court in this respect is translated hereinbelow:

> For going to make peace with the tribes neighboring on New Mexico (Memoir to the Sieur de Bourgmont approved by His Royal Highness).
>
> Sieur de Bourgmont, whom the Company of the Indies has nominated to establish a post on the Missouri River in Louisiana and to command there, consents to depart on this expedition, on conditions that have been offered to him, after having been approved by His Royal Highness: he is to be paid his salary since August 12, 1719, the date of his commission, and on his arrival in Louisiana a gratuity of 2,000 livres in merchandise.
>
> He represents that the services he has rendered, as well in Canada as in Louisiana, have merited him the Cross of St. Louis from His Royal Highness, and as the difficulties which he will undergo and the dangers to which he will be exposed in execution of his enterprise cannot be recompensed by money, he hopes, that if he is fortunate enough to succeed, that His Royal Highness will afford him a title of nobility, which is the sole favor that he expects for this important service he renders in going to make a peace with all the Indian tribes settled in Louisiana and New Mexico, to secure the way to voyageurs, and to establish a post which will protect the mines of Illinois from the designs of the Spanish and open to the French a very advantageous trade by land with them. [These] things cannot be executed more promptly nor with more ease by anyone, according to the opinions of the Commandants of the colony.
>
> Approved by Signature of His Royal Highness.

This condition was accepted and his commission as Commandant of the Missouri based upon this understanding, read as follows:

Instructions give[n] to Sieur de Bourgmont, Commandant of the Missouri, for the Mission which he must complete:

His Royal Highness having approved the commission given by the Company of the Indies to Sieur de Bourgmont to assume the command on the Missouri River and to establish there a post, he will without delay proceed to L'Orient in order to embark on the first vessel sailing to Louisiana.

On his arrival in that colony he will receive the orders of M. de Bienville, general commandant, and take his instructions for proceeding to his destination and for executing there those things which will advance the welfare of the service to the King and to the Company of the Indies.

He will request the said Sieur de Bienville and the Council of Colonies to speed his expedition by refurnishing him promptly the material necessary for his expedition and the projected establishment.

He will then proceed to Illinois as soon as possible where on his arrival, he will receive the orders of M. de Boisbriant, the first Lieutenant of the King of the Colony, concerning the site where he is to establish the post on the Missouri River, upon the course he is to pursue in regard to the Indian tribes, and the proper conditions under which he will make peace treaties with them.

The said Sieur de Boisbriant will give him an order and instructions in writing and sign them in duplicate, one of which the said M. de Boisbriant shall forward to us.

The said Sieur de Bourgmont knows well enough the principal object of a post on the Missouri is to approach the Spaniards, especially to establish commercial relations with them, and meanwhile fortify the post to be established in order to be able to maintain it against them in case of rupture. He cannot be too careful in the choice of a location where the establishment is to be founded, for on its situation success of the enterprise is dependent.

He also knows the importance of inducing the Co-manches to enter into a treaty of peace with all Indian tribes allied with the French. He will spare no endeavor to bring this about, since this is one of the principal objects of his expedition.

After having made the said establishment and effected an alliance with the Comanches, we order M. de Boisbriant that the said Sieur de Bourgmont shall engage several chiefs of the principal nations to accompany him to France, in order to give them an idea of the French power and the said Sieur de Boisbriant and the Council of the Colonies will provide all that is necessary for this purpose.

If the said Sieur de Bourgmont is successful in carrying out the agreement into which he has entered with the Company and whereof mention has been made heretofore within a period of two years, as he has promised, the Council will without interference permit his return to France, and he will enjoy the favors promised by His Royal Highness. But it will be necessary for him to bring a certificate from M. de Boisbriant and the Council of the Colonies reporting that he has established a strong fort on the Missouri and that he has effected a treaty of peace between the Comanches and those savage tribes who are at war with French allies.

Done at Paris the 17th day of January 1722

Signed Fagon, Ferrand, Machault, and Dodun

This document is itself an interesting reflection of the Regency. Dated during Orleans' tenure, it was signed by the Council including Fagon (apparently Louis XIV's old physician) and by Machault, later to become high in Louis XV's financial circles. It shows the lingering money problems of the Company of the Indies, since Bourgmont had not been paid since 1719 and also didn't trust the Company or the Council to come through on the promise of 2,000 livres for merchandise unless he received it in specie in France. The late hostilities with Spain bubbled just below the surface, and a "rupture" of relations was considered a possibility.

Bourgmont was directed to leave France in January, 1722, but he didn't actually depart from Paris until June of that year. When he got to New Orleans, he was met with the first of many trying experiences which were to confront him. Nothing whatever had been done in furtherance of the orders from France to prepare for his major expedition upriver. But he persevered and finally got men and materials organized and proceeded via Fort de Chartres where he enlisted an associate, St. Ange de Bellerieve, to accompany him to the Missouri River. There in 1723 (during the winter!) he built his little stockade fort on the north side of the river across from the Missouri Indian villages, near the present town of Brunswick in what is now Carroll County, Missouri. Its site was selected by Engineer Renaudiere, the same gentleman who chose the location for the later Fort Cavagnial (and who, significantly, also liked the location at Kawsmouth where Kansas City was later located, calling the Kansas a "beautiful river"!). Bourgmont named the post Fort Orleans in honor of the Regent. A large highway historical marker now commemorates Fort Orleans (and an older stone marker is nearby).

Fort Orleans was a perfect textbook example of a little French colonial frontier fort. A plan of the fort found in fairly recent years by Baron Villiers shows it to have been constructed on the general plan of Louis XIV's great military engineer, Marshal Vauban, i.e., with curtain walls on about a 100-foot square and, at each corner, bastions designed to direct an enfilade fire against attackers advancing toward the walls. Bourgmont's own journals and letters indicate that the soldiers first built their own barracks and later (in December) finished the fortification and bastions and the warehouse, as well as a church and cottage for the resident priest, Father Mercier. Bourgmont noted that many of his soldiers and all of his "sailors" had deserted along the way and that the workmen were lazy—a not atypical occurrence since the Company of the Indies had resorted to literally kidnapping young men (and occasionally women) to become workers in the Mississippi Valley and its tributaries. Eventually there were also (according to Villiers' map) an icehouse, small gardens, a field of tobacco, a kitchen garden, fields where the soldiers planted crops, and a powder magazine in one of the bastions of the fort.

While Bourgmont lived for a time in an Indian hut, he eventually moved to a house of plain unsquared logs (probably upright *poteaux en terre*) with a thatched roof. To make the house more comfortable, the logs were covered with a plaster called *bousillage,* a mixture of clay and straw. The officers' houses appearing on the plan located by Baron Villiers look quite substantial, but it is somewhat doubtful they were ever built. Fort Orleans had the distinction of appearing on a number of contemporary maps (although in confusingly different locations). St. Ange may have been its commandant during part of its occupancy. From it, Bourgmont would conduct his agreed-upon trip to open up a way through the Comanche country for French trade with New Mexico—a harbinger of the Santa Fe Trail.

On June 25, 1724, part of Bourgmont's entourage set out by water from Fort Orleans for the Kansa village on the first leg of his epic journey to the Padoucas (Plains Comanches). Since they represent (aside from Le Sueur and Commandant de Bourgmont) the first known Europeans to have traversed the immediate Kansas City area, I shall quote the first few sentences of their journal:

> Departure from Fort Orleans Sunday, June 25, 1724. The detachment left this noon by water for the Canzes and from there for the Padoucas. Commander is Mr. de Saint-Ange, ensign of the Fort Orleans, with Dubois, Sergeant, Rotisseur and Gentil, corporals, and eleven soldiers, to wit: La Jeunesse, Bonneau, Saint Lazare, Ferret, Derbet, Avignon,

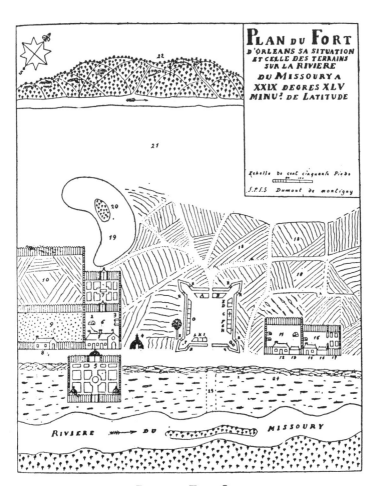

PLAN OF FORT ORLEANS

Its location and that of the lands on the river of the Missouri
at XXXIX degrees XLV minutes of latitude.

Scale: one hundred and fifty feet.

Explanation of the alphabetical letters: A, Commandant's house. B, Officers' house.
C, Chapel. D, Blacksmith's house. E, Forge. F, Chaplain's house. G, Storekeeper's
house. H, Store. I, Guard-house. K, Drummer's house. L, Laundry. O, Barracks.
P, Flag-staff. Q, Powder magazine. R, Embrasures for the cannon.

Explanation of the figures: 1, M. DeBourgmont's house. 2, His poultry-house. 3, His
oven. 4, Ice-house. 5, Big garden. 6, His yard. 7, Little garden. 8, Store. 9, Field of
tobacco. 10, Plot used as a kitchen-garden. 11, M. St. Ange's yard. 12, His house.
13, Storeroom. 14, House of M. St. Ange, *fils*, officer. 15, Storeroom. 16, His yard.
17, Little garden. 18, Soldiers' field. 19, Pond. 20, Island. 21, Prairie. 22, Big hills
two leagues distant from the fort. 23, Road from the river to the fort. 24, Little em-
bankment fifteen feet high.

Plan of Fort Orleans, drawn by Dumont de Montigny (*Mid-America*,
January 1930, p. 259). Courtesy of Kansas City Public Library.

Sans Chagrin, Poupard, Gaspard, Chalons, and Brasseur;
five Canadians: Mercier (a priest), Quesnel, Rivet, Rolet
and Lespine, and two men engaged by Mr. Renaudiere,
Touluse and Antoine.

It is generally assumed, from both internal and external
evidence, that de Renaudiere, Ingénieur des Mines, one of the
two men with scientific training in the party, wrote the journal
of the expedition. The other professional was Surgeon Quesnel, the first doctor to set foot in Kansas City! Concerning the
men in the overland group, Renaudiere wrote:

On Monday, July 3, Mr. de Bourgmont left overland,
accompanied by Mr. de Renaudiere and Bellerieve, Es-
tienne, Roulot and Derbet, cadets in the army, and a
drummer Hamelin, Canadian, Gaillard enlisted by Mr.
Renaudiere and Simon, valet of Mr. de Bourgmont, with a
hundred Missouri Indians, commanded by eight war chiefs
and the big chief of the nation, and sixty-four Osages
commanded by four war chiefs of their nation.

Also accompanying Bourgmont on horseback, but not
mentioned in these lists, was his young son by his Missouri
Indian wife.

We have a detailed day-by-day, and almost league-by-
league, account of the overland journey, since Renaudiere, the
reporter, was with that group. The courses and distances
which he sets out show that the party traversed northern Clay
and Platte counties along the northern edge of the present city
limits of Kansas City and held a formal palaver with the
Kansa advance party on the high ground several miles east of
Weston, Missouri, in Platte County on Thursday, July 6, 1724.
On their journey they had encountered "great heat" and saw
"several turkeys," "hazelnut trees laden with hazelnuts," and
deer "in herds." The pow-wow held by the Kansa for Bourgmont, almost within sight of the tall buildings in present
downtown Kansas City (and not far from Kansas City

International Airport), deserves mention:

> They (the Kansa) received him and the French, who were
> with him, waving the peace pipe in the air, with great joy.
> After having smoked the peace pipe with the French, they
> spread the war mat and prepared a banquet with several
> kinds of meat, all of which they had prepared, and they also
> received the Osages and the Missouris, we camped there on
> the height of the prairie. They all danced and made
> fireworks with muskets.

On Friday the seventh the expedition reached the Missouri
and on Saturday they crossed it in the Weston vicinity and
went to the Kansa village for feasts and speeches. (This was the
village just north of present Fort Leavenworth at which a
priest was located in 1727 and at which Fort Cavagnial was
built in 1744.)

All we know about the party traveling by water is that they
arrived at the Kansa village a few days after they set out. Since
they only traveled by day, we can assume that they may have
spent at least one night somewhere in the vicinity of Kawsmouth. Certain it is that they viewed the bluffs, the big bend in
the Missouri, and the Kansas River entering from the south, as
Bourgmont had done a few years before.

It was well into fall before all of the preparations could be
made for the final journey on to the Comanches. Renaudiere
gives us this picturesque commentary on the start of the
expedition:

> We left at six o'clock in the morning with beating drum and
> waving flag, arms and baggage. When reaching the village,
> we took battle formation and afterwards the drummer
> began to drum the march and we started to march.

The French, 32 in number, were accompanied by around
1,000 Indians, all told. This was without doubt the most
impressive panoply that Kansas—or the entire central plains
region—had seen since Coronado. What a fitting subject for a

painting! (It bears mention that Coronado's hasty trip into Kansas was made with a picked cadre of only a handful of mounted men and lasted only a few brief days.)

During the early part of the trip the expedition saw herds of buffalo containing so many head it was impossible to count them. Bourgmont demonstrated his prowess by shooting a buffalo from horseback. Unfortunately, however, he was struck down by fever and grew rapidly worse. He was so determined to reach his objective that he commanded that a litter be made and was carried onward, semi-delirious, for several days. Surgeon Quesnel must have had his hands full at this critical time. Bourgmont's strength and all vestige of rationality gave out, and he was returned past present-day Kansas City to Fort Orleans.

While an advance party under Gaillard went ahead to make assurances to the Comanches, Bourgmont recuperated at the fort and on September 20, 1724 was again ready to set out. He left Fort Orleans September 20, traveling by water past the now-familiar sights at Kawsmouth, and reached the friendly Kansa village on October 2, 1724. On the eighth he left for the Comanches, arriving there (near present Ellsworth, Kansas) on October 18. There a great drama was unfolded as Bourgmont made harangue after harangue, heaping up presents for the assembled chiefs of the Comanches and their people. The chiefs in turn sought to impress him with their power, the number of braves they controlled, and the extent of their territory. They averred that the presents of the Spanish were but trifles compared to the munificence of the French and that they would be friends and allies of the French and allow their traders free access to the lands of the Spanish, to Taos and Santa Fe, only several days distant. But for the delay caused by his illness, Bourgmont would surely have been able to go on to New Mexico. It was a remarkable feat for Bourgmont to get the Comanches to even talk to himself and the chiefs of the more easterly tribes, since the latter had been at war with the Comanches and frequently sold them into slavery. Bourgmont had to stifle the French pressure for more slaves, promise the Missouri River tribes better trade privileges in lieu of the slave trade, and get them to assure the Comanches that they would henceforth live in peace with them. This is actually an oversimplification of the problem, and Bourgmont neatly balanced the cravings and animosities of an astonishingly large number of Indians and Frenchmen in order to achieve his final treaty.

Bourgmont left the Comanche camp on October 22, 1724, and journeyed triumphantly once more past, or near, the future site of Kansas City, arriving at Fort Orleans on November 5. There he had Father Mercier celebrate the victorious expedition by singing the "Te Deum" in the little post chapel—the first such service on the Missouri River.

True to his bargain to deliver influential Indians to Paris, Bourgmont left the next year for Paris with several Indian chiefs (including the famous Chicagou, after whom Chicago is named) and a princess of the Missouri tribe. On September 20, 1725, they arrived in Paris. Bourgmont and his entourage were royally entertained at receptions given by the Duke and Duchess de Bourbon and by the directors of the Company of the Indies. The King even held a special audience for them. Sergeant Dubois married the princess of the Missouris in Notre Dame Cathedral (after the Duchess of Orleans stood as her godmother at her baptism). The entire party did war dances on stage at the Opera and had a hunt, using deer as quarry, in the Bois de Boulogne. Chief Chicagou observed to the Duchess d'Orleans that he hoped that she would be "fertile with many warriors" as her husband's family (the Bourbons) had been. Another chief told the writer Bossu 28 years afterwards that while at the Tuileries and elsewhere he had seen "men who were half women, with curled hair, earrings, and corsages on their chests." (This was at the height of the foppish Regency period when the dandies dressed in exactly the manner he described.) He concluded that he was sure they wore rouge, and that in his opinion they "smelled like alligators." The

Duchess d'Orleans gave Chief Chicagou a snuff box which he
treasured for the rest of his life. One wonders where it is now.
The fifteen-year-old King gave the princess of the Missouris a
wedding present of a repeating watch set with diamonds. The
Indians thought it was supernatural because its movement
seemingly never ceased.

Bossu also asked another chief in the party what he felt was
beautiful in Paris (the interview taking place in America 28
years after the event):

> He replied that the Rue des Boucheries was beautiful
> because of the quantity of meat he had seen there, and that
> the Rue Saint Honoré pleased him, too. . . . When he told
> (his friends) that he had seen the great village of the French
> . . . as many people as there are leaves on the trees of their
> forest . . . they answered that, since such a thing was im-
> possible, the Europeans must have bewitched his eyes and
> must have shown him the same people over and over again.
> He added that he had seen the cabins of the great French
> chiefs, Versailles and the Louvre, and that they held more
> people than there were in all the tribal lands. He said that he
> had also seen the cabin of the old warriors, l'Hôtel Royal des
> Invalides. Since the old man was beginning to be senile, he
> agreed with the other Indians that the French must have
> bewitched him.

Regarding the peregrinations of Bourgmont and his troupe,
it has been suggested somewhat uncharitably, though perhaps
accurately, that he put on the very first "Wild West Show" to
drum up interest in the affairs of the sagging Company of the
Indies. As interest dropped off, the Indians were left to their
own devices and became almost poverty stricken, finally being
sent home by charitable donations. Sergeant Dubois and his
wife, Mme. Dubois, the princess of the Missouris, apparently
returned to the vicinity of Fort Orleans after returning from
Paris, but he died shortly thereafter and she married Monsieur
"Mavin." Mavin (Marin) obtained the permission of the

Company of the Indies to trade with the Missouris (and Kansas) in 1728 and kept it until 1736, when it was revoked by the company. It was probably he who was reported to be shipping cattle from the Missouris' area to St. Louis in the 1730s. After that all reports of activity in the vicinity of old Fort Orleans cease, although Villiers, a modern French historian, thought it may have been active through the 1730s and 1740s. He probably confused the later reports of Fort Cavagnial with Fort Orleans, however.

Bourgmont, on the other hand, received the promised title of nobility and returned to the rich widow of gentle birth whom he had married before leaving France. He never returned to America, and for that matter he seems to have retired from public life in France. He is said to have died in about 1730. The heraldic coat of arms given to him by the King's authority (designed by Charles d'Hozier, his Master of Heraldry) in a way symbolizes what he achieved in mid-America—the first open route from the Missouri River to the mountains. It shows a plains Indian against a background of silver mountains (the Rockies) under an azure sky. So far as we know, this is the only European armorial device earned in, and portraying, the trans-Missouri area.

Some writers are at pains to demonstrate that Bourgmont's expedition and the treaty he negotiated were mere useless gestures leaving no tangible results. This is hardly an accurate statement of fact and illustrates the penalty mid-Americans have to pay for letting outsiders write their own indigenous history. The very fact that Bourgmont did what he did when he did is of considerable importance to Midwestern history, entirely apart from any value judgments respecting what he may have accomplished. As to the latter, who is there who will say that the first man in history to open up the trail for safe passage from Kawsmouth to Taos and Santa Fe should not receive our attention and accolades? The publicity attendant upon his successful return ensured a permanent place for the trail to Santa Fe in the minds of Europeans and the Yankees to

the east. His was a significant feat, accomplished in the face of
official inertia and intermeddling, sickness, the elements, and
the chameleon-like loyalties of the Indians. True, it may not
compare in scope with the expeditions of Marquette and
Joliet, or La Salle, but it was at least of considerable regional
importance. We have no way of knowing how soon and in
what numbers the French traders availed themselves of the
route which Bourgmont had opened, but we know that some
at least made the attempt. Even though Fort Orleans was
abandoned by the Company of the Indies in about 1729,
Father Mercier was still there until the mid-1730s, and it may
have been occupied by St. Ange and traders from time to time
almost up until the opening of Fort Cavagnial higher up the
Missouri River in 1744.

We do know of one celebrated expedition to Santa Fe in
1739, the success of which may have been due to the residual
goodwill left among the Comanches from Bourgmont's expedition. This was the trip made by the Mallet brothers, Pierre
and Paul, and eight or nine others, up the Missouri (past
whatever was left of Fort Orleans and the site of present
Kansas City) to the Platte, up that river to the Comanche
country, then overland across Nebraska and northwestern
Kansas, Colorado and New Mexico to Santa Fe. As a result of
the success of the Mallet expedition, a number of others, some
successful and some not, were undertaken. Although the trips
to Santa Fe were frequently of limited success due to official
Spanish opposition, there was from Bourgmont's time until
the end of French occupation a lively, and lucrative, French
trade at the pueblos (particularly Taos) and Indian villages on
the northeastern periphery of the area of Spanish settlement.
This was, in effect, the real beginning of what eventually
became the Santa Fe Trail. Bourgmont, in fact, was the
putative "Father of the Santa Fe Trail," but it was his
misfortune to have been a Frenchman and therefore a non-
person from the standpoint of American history.

Perhaps Bourgmont deserves to be remembered by Kansas

Citians, if for no other reason, because of the following high compliment paid in his journal to the general plains area from Kansas City westward:

> This is the finest country and the most beautiful land in the world; the prairies are like the seas, and filled with wild animals; especially oxen, cattle, hind and stag in such quantities to surpass the imagination.

Bourgmont was Kansas City's La Salle, yet no park preserves his memory, no hotel bears his proud and fine-sounding name, no statue bears his likeness, no Bourgmont Bridge spans his beloved Missouri River. Some day Kansas City may find a way to return the compliment by commemorating the remarkable accomplishments, two and one-half centuries ago, of its first definitely known European visitor, Captain Etienne Veniard, Sieur de Bourgmont, Commandant of the Missouri, Chevalier of the Royal and Military Order of St. Louis.

CHAPTER III

Fort de Cavagnial

VERSAILLES, APRIL 25, 1746. The palace of Louis XIV, the Sun King, was occupied by his successor and great-grandson Louis XV and the latter's unofficial prime minister, Madame de Pompadour. Jean Frederick Phelipeaux, Comte de Maurepas, Minister of Colonies, writing to the Marquis de Vaudreuil, Governor of Louisiana, directed him in the name of the King to "complete the fort which has been begun" on the Missouri River. Some even say that Pompadour authorized the post.

The object of this attention by the court of *Vieille France* was the westernmost of the several French forts in the "Illinois country" of Upper Louisiana. This incredible little *présence française* in Kansas was located on rising ground overlooking the village of the Kansa Indians on Salt Creek, opposite Kickapoo Island in present Leavenworth County, Kansas, just north of the Fort Leavenworth boundary. The fort consisted of a stockade of stout piles, 80 feet on the inside square, with bastions at each corner in the classic Vauban style, the rear bastions being "storied." It compared roughly in both size and manner of construction with Fort Duquesne in western Pennsylvania except for outworks. We know nothing to date concerning the details of its armament, if any. Inside were a commandant's house, a guard house, a powder house (all with an upper story), a traders' house, and a house for the employees of the traders. The buildings were of logs and most were covered with mud *(bousillage)*, and had chimneys also made of mud over logs.

Governor Vaudreuil-Cavagnial had practically finalized his plans for the post in the summer of 1743, for he wrote to Maurepas, Minister of Colonies, of a "small fort" which should be built in the Missouri country. He advised that he had already laid the foundation for a company which would be charged with the "building and repairing of a fort and lodgings convenient for this small troop, also with the transporting of all necessaries for their subsistence and convenience." In Governor Vaudreuil's letter to Minister Maurepas of August 30, 1744, after repeating his oft-stated reasons for establishing the Missouri post (mainly curbing the abuses of the rascally Canadian coureurs de bois), he stated that in the spring (1744) he had commenced construction of the post and had named it "Fort de la Trinite." He then went on to describe in detail the terms of the trader's license which were the same as those set out in his ordinance of August 8, 1744 naming one Deruisseau as the trader at Fort Trinite. But the name for the fort modestly chosen by the governor didn't stick. All the later references to it (and there are many) use "Cavagnial" with one spelling or another, in honor of the governor who founded the post.

The commanding situation of the fort was not chosen fortuitously. Governor Vaudreuil, in the instrument authorizing the fort, directed that it was to be built at the location selected by one La Gautrais. The Chevalier Pierre Rene Harpin de la Gautrais was an experienced military engineer who had worked extensively in Louisiana on permanent fortifications, as well as in the field. At the time he selected the site for Fort de Cavagnial (1744) he held the rank of lieutenant and, as special envoy and engineer for the Louisiana governor, was engaged in a detailed survey of the Missouri from its confluence with the Mississippi to near the Platte, including the preparation of a relief map of this part of the river. He was thus eminently qualified to make the choice of a location. The wisdom of this choice was confirmed by the location in 1827 of Fort Leavenworth in roughly the same position on the west

François-Pierre Rigaud, Baron de Cavagnial, Marquis de Vaudreuil.

bluffs only two and one-half miles downstream. La Gautrais, incidentally, was not the first French engineer to survey the Missouri. Bourgmont and his party had done so in 1714, and La Renaudiere, Ingénieur des Mines, surveyed all available sites, including Kawsmouth, in deciding upon a location for Fort Orleans in 1723.

The fort was officially chartered on August 8, 1744. With the King's consent, an influential trader, one Deruisseau, was granted all trading rights on the Missouri River and its tributaries from January 1, 1745, to May 20, 1750, with the fort as his headquarters.

On December 6, 1744, Vaudreuil wrote to Maurepas enclosing a copy of this "trade agreement" granted on August 8, 1744, to "M. de Deruisseau Voyageur of Canada whose honesty is known to me." The purposes stated in the authorizing order, the full text of which is fortunately extant (see Appendix A) were to control the unruly Canadian *voyageurs* and coureurs de bois in their fur trade with the Indians, to discover mines and minerals, and to "penetrate from that place at the end [sic] of the Missouri even as far as Santa Fe itself, in order to discover the exact location of the route, and in order to be able later to establish trade easily with the Spaniards"—i.e., to establish a Santa Fe trail.

We now know that Deruisseau was not merely an "absentee landlord" with a sinecure at Fort de Cavagnial. He seems to have been personally involved with on-site work in constructing the trading post. On March 15, 1747, Governor Vaudreuil advised the minister that information arriving from Bertet (Commandant at the Illinois) included a report that Deruisseau, during the previous spring, was "working hard to finish the fort which His Majesty has approved that he build on the Missouri River." Vaudreuil added his own comments on how effective this and other measures had been in curbing the abuses and disorders which had been rampant on the Missouri due to "vagabonds and coureurs de bois." Somewhat prophetically, he added that such unsavory characters "often occasioned us desertions." They were not entirely eliminated, for Commandant La Barre, the Governor's own protege and cousin-in-law, would soon be murdered by a deserting soldier made drunk on illicit brandy sold by two of them.

But why a French fort right among the Kansa? The reason was simple: furs. This was basically a trading fort, and the French-speaking Kansa were customers, not enemies. With few exceptions, the French in these early years did not trap for furs; rather, they traded guns, tools, cooking utensils, trinkets, and cloth goods to the Indians in return for them. To get the furs the French had to go where the Indians were. Thus, from the second old Kansa village (near present Doniphan in the early 1700s), to Fort de Cavagnial at the first old Kansa village in the mid-1700s, to Chouteau's camp at Kawsmouth (serving the final Kansa encampment in Kansas, upstream near present Topeka), the French-speaking traders moved their base of operations to keep in close contact with the peripatetic Kansa nation.

The Kansa were known as a major tribe to Europeans from the early years and hence had been an object of French interest almost from the first days of Mississippi Valley exploration. Coronado's scouts, in 1541, reported on the Gaues (Kaws) who were probably located at that early date somewhere near the later site of the fort. It is said that Fr. Juan de Padilla, the devoted Franciscan, was on his way to carry the Gospel to the Kaws when he was martyred in 1542.

As discussed in Chapter I, Père Marquette, although he did not ascend the Missouri, interviewed Indians as he descended and later ascended the Mississippi in 1673 (passing the mouth of the Missouri in the process) and prepared a map on which he accurately located the "Kansa." Frontenac, probably the greatest governor of New France, was the prime mover in the discovery and development of the Illinois country, even going so far as to violate his official orders in giving encouragement to such men as Marquette, Joliet, and La Salle. It was La Salle who in 1682 claimed all of "Louisiana," including most of present Kansas, for France. Father Marc Bergier, appointed vicar-general by the bishop at Quebec and superior of the seminary (of Quebec) missionaries in the Mississippi Valley, and one of the earliest residents of the Illinois country, wrote in May, 1702, that if he had the men and resources he would very much have liked to establish a mission to the "Cancez" (Kansa). On June 20 of the same year, Pierre le Moyne, Sieur d'Iberville, founder and first governor of Louisiana, wrote that the Kansa tribe had a population of 1,500.

French interest in the tribes of the Missouri Valley area, including the Kansa, was heightened by the armed Spanish

expedition led by Villasur into the Pawnee country in 1720
and by the first scientifically conducted and reported reconnaissance of the Missouri from the Mississippi to the Platte,
conducted by Bourgmont, in 1714. Bourgmont, in writing his
report, had referred to the "Ecanze" as "ally and friend of the
French." So they remained for over a century.

Bienville, an early governor of Louisiana, had urged the
construction of a fort on the Missouri as early as 1719, and the
next year his views were seconded by Boisbriant, the commandant of the Illinois country. The idea of a fort near the Kansa
gained impetus; indeed it had some historical precedent.
Bourgmont, while on one of his expeditions, had established a
"fortified camp" adjacent to Kansa territory on Isle au Vache
(Cow Island) near present Iatan, Missouri, north of Fort
Leavenworth. Due to the vagaries of the Missouri, that
"island" has from time to time actually been a part of the
Kansas "mainland."

As we have seen, the man picked to construct the new fort
(Orleans), which was destined to be the downstream predecessor of Cavagnial, was Bourgmont, whose exploits in founding
Fort Orleans and getting a peace treaty with the Comanches
we have noted in Chapter II. Fort Orleans soon began to fall
into disrepair, and it was abandoned in 1728 or 1729. With the
fort gone, matters went from bad to worse for French traders
on the Missouri. Governor Bienville wrote on July 25, 1733,
that in the preceding winter the Indians on the Missouri had
killed eleven French *voyageurs.* Benoist de St. Claire, second in
command at Fort Chartres, headquarters for the Illinois
country, wrote in 1740 that due to lack of contact he was
unable to report on the affairs of the *voyageurs* among the tribes
on the Missouri. Those Canadian traders who did chance the
Missouri area were so unruly that even the Indians asked that
they be curbed.

The situation was clearly ripe for re-establishing the French
position on the Missouri. The event which provided the final
impetus was the expedition of the Mallet brothers which

successfully reached Santa Fe via the Missouri and Platte rivers and a final overland journey. The French thereupon determined to establish a base of operations which could serve not only as a control point for the fur trade with the Indians, but also as a point of departure for trade with the Spaniards in Santa Fe and Taos.

The Kansa village met both needs admirably. The friendly Kansa were a prolific source of high-grade furs, and their village on Salt Creek (known as the village of 12—i.e., 12 leagues from the mouth of the Kansas River) was on both the river-overland route and the relatively untried direct land route to Santa Fe. For many years they had dealt with the French at their old village of 24 (i.e., 24 leagues from the mouth of the Kansas) near Doniphan. Sometime before 1744 they moved all of their people from the latter location to the village downstream, which thereafter took over the designation of grand village. Hence it was that the then governor of Louisiana, Vaudreuil-Cavagnial, signed at New Orleans on August 8, 1744, the previously mentioned ordinance which directed the completion of a fort already begun "at the Kansas on the Missouri River."

Although the fort was referred to initially as simply the "Post on the Missouri," and by Governor Vaudreuil as "Fort de la Trinite," it appears soon to have been given, quite appropriately, the name of the governor who had planned it and given it its legal birth: i.e., Cavagnial, sometimes incorrectly spelled *Cavagnal,* and more recently *Cavagnolle.* The governor himself signed his name *Cavagnial.* This governor was none other than François-Pierre Rigaud, Baron de Cavagnial, Marquis de Vaudreuil, son of a former governor-general of New France, and himself destined to be Louis XV's last governor and lieutenant-general in New France. It is difficult to avoid name-dropping when speaking of Vaudreuil. Castle Vaudreuil in coastal Normandy, the family home, was built by his Norman ancestors on the site of a Roman fort, and William the Conqueror spent his boyhood there.

Fregault, in his well-known book, *Le Grand Marquis,* does not associate the "post on the Missouri," which he discusses at some length, with the name of Cavagnial, although he describes its planning and establishment by Governor Vaudreuil. He nevertheless helps to confirm the propriety of this association. He shows that there was only one Cavagnial of note—the governor—so-named by his father after one of the family estates in Languedoc in southern France in order to distinguish him from other members of the family Vaudreuil. After his father's death and his own rise to prominence, however, he ceased to be Monsieur de Cavagnial and used the old family name of Vaudreuil.

Vaudreuil-Cavagnial was awarded the Grand Cross of the Royal and Military Order of St. Louis in 1730. As a youth in the Canadian "troupes de la Marine" (so-called because they, like all regular French colonial forces, were administered by the navy) he had advanced rapidly through the officer ranks. He was commissary under de Ligneris in the major campaign against the Fox Indians in 1728 and governor of Three Rivers (next in size after Quebec and Montreal) from 1733 to 1742. He returned to France for about a year and returned in 1743 as governor of Louisiana where he served until 1753. He was a commanding personage of the very best political, military, and social connections, conducted an effective and conscientious administration, and was and is still remembered in Louisiana as "Le Grand Marquis."

Vaudreuil returned to France after his long sojourn in Louisiana, only to return in 1755, with a great convoy, as Governor-General of all New France—a New France whose star was fast falling. He was the supreme commander-in-chief of that country, superior in authority even to General Montcalm. His problems with the peculations of the Intendant Bigot and the impetuous Montcalm are too familiar and involved to recount here, as are the criticisms leveled at Vaudreuil himself. Suffice it to say that the namesake of Fort Cavagnial, in the dying days of his county's largest colony, carried out the orders of his King in the face of great opposition and under overwhelmingly trying circumstances. He surrendered Montreal to the British in 1760 and died in Paris on August 4, 1778.

But to return to the history of the fort, it will be recalled that it was established by Vaudreuil's ordinance in 1744. The trade to be supervised by the fort was of the *congé* or license type, and one Joseph Deruisseau was by the ordinance given the privilege of controlling all trade on the Missouri and its tributaries from January 1, 1745, until May 20, 1750. He was authorized to grant licenses to others, who in turn would set up lesser trading posts and "little forts" among the several tribes. The commandant of the fort was to keep the peace, secure to the *congé* the enjoyment of his exclusive license, and was to be paid by a levy upon the traders. Thus it will be seen that Fort de Cavagnial was the commercial and military center of a vast territory in mid-America, supervising a number of subposts throughout the region. Most of the present states of Missouri, Kansas, and Nebraska were in fact under its jurisdiction, and in theory so were many others, although the French did not actually progress much beyond the Platte to the north and the authority of other French forts overlapped to the east and south. The Comanche barrier and the Spaniards set its western limits.

Deruisseau's full name appears to have been Joseph Trottier LeFebvre d'Inglebert Deruisseau, and due to the rather scrambled orthography practiced at that time, his last name was sometimes shown as "des Bruisseau." He was born in France, went to Louisiana with Governor Vaudreuil, accompanied by his wife and infant son, and in 1743 was in New Orleans where he was given his trade concession. He seems also to have had a seigniory at L'isle Perrot in Canada. In 1744 he went up the Mississippi to Fort de Chartres and, from there presumably for a time, to Fort de Cavagnial, where his term as *congé* appears to have coincided with Villiers' tour as commandant. After his license expired in 1750, or perhaps even before,

Deruisseau was at Fort de Chartres where he took up residence, became quite prominent, and served as commissary, King's storekeeper, and judge of civil cases for a number of years. Both Commandant St. Ange and Judge LeFebvre-Deruisseau signed the *procès verbal* turning over legal title to Fort de Chartres to the English. When St. Ange and the judge surrendered the fort and removed the seat of French authority to St. Louis in 1765, Deruisseau went there and served as civil judge until his death. One of his cases is reported in Billon's *Annals of St. Louis.* It involved the impounding of the goods of a trader who had been captured by the Indians. Judge Deruisseau, the notary, and the attorney in the "Royal jurisdiction of Illinois" duly went to Ste. Genevieve to examine witnesses, view and inventory the goods, and place them in protective custody, "after maturely considering the circumstances." Judge Deruisseau also participated with St. Ange in the first fifteen of the early real estate transactions in St. Louis, later to become known as the "Spanish titles." Thereafter, as "Keeper of the King's Warehouse" he was in charge of the military stores brought over from Fort Chartres. His son, Pierre François, married Margaret de la Ferne, the daughter of the surgeon-major at Fort de Chartres. The senior Deruisseau died on April 3, 1767, at St. Louis, after many years of service to the French in the Illinois country. His estate inventory listed a very substantial amount of military stores (left to St. Ange's care) demonstrating his faithful stewardship as the King's storekeeper.

In the interest of historical accuracy, it should be pointed out parenthetically that there is no express written documentation that "Deruisseau's fort" was identical with the "Fort on the Missouri"—i.e., Fort de Cavagnial. Since his authorization was from Governor Vaudreuil-Cavagnial, it seems logical that his fort is the one which came to be called Cavagnial—and unlikely that any other in the area would be so called. There is no contrary evidence; the French continued to maintain and garrison a fort at the Kansa village, and no new construction, at a different location, is mentioned in the rather voluminous set of reports between Vaudreuil and the Illinois commandants. There is certainly no indication that there were *two* Missouri posts. It may, therefore, be assumed that they were one and the same. The fort would have been left in quite usable condition after only five years of occupancy under Deruisseau's lease, and money for new forts was hard to come by in the Illinois district.

Fort Cavagnial's interesting day-to-day activity can be partially reconstructed from the records. The fort was situated on rising ground about a mile inland from the large Kansa Indian village. The village itself was located immediately on the river bank in a valley between two high bluffs (still very prominent features of the landscape) and probably presented an interesting view from the fort. There was a fine spring flowing into a little stream near the fort, from which fresh water was obtained. We know that horses were kept at the fort, so there was probably a corral or stable either within or adjacent to it. Also, as previously noted, the garrison or the traders kept cows on an island near the fort. It is probable that provision gardens, a tobacco field, and kitchen gardens similar to the ones kept at Fort Orleans were also kept at Cavagnial. In 1746 a Mémoire on Louisiana stated there were 20 Frenchmen and 10 slaves at the Missouri post, and that they were engaged in hunting and trading and raised corn and tobacco.

The Illinois was one of nine "districts" of Louisiana, the latter being administered like a "department" of France. Missouri, as all of Fort de Cavagnial's jurisdiction was called, was administered as a sort of subdistrict of Illinois. The habitants were governed by the code of ordinances known as the "Custom of Paris," and the soldiers at the posts were governed by the naval regulations, they being "troupes de la Marine."

It would be a mistake to picture Cavagnial as an isolated post in the midst of hostile aborigines in a vast unexplored wilderness. Western exploration and history did not begin with Lewis and Clark, and Pike, as some might believe. The Missouri, Kansa, and Pawnee had been allies of the French since early in the 1700s, and *voyageurs* in sizable numbers had long been trading with them, intermarrying with them, and exploring their territory, starting even before the turn of the century. These tribes spoke French and used French firearms, tools, cloth goods, and cooking utensils. They had come to rely so much on these trade goods that their occasional short supply was a serious hardship and cause for complaint. The French, on the other hand, avidly sought the furs which the tribes collected. Many were converted, or at least exposed, to Christianity. Fort Orleans, not far down the river, and Bourgmont's diplomacy with the Missouri there had paved the way for good relations. Except for wintertime, the Missouri River was a veritable highway at the door of the fort, carrying traffic at least as far as the Platte, and possibly beyond. All four quarters of Kansas had been penetrated by well-organized expeditions—the joint French-Jumano trips across the southwest and into Colorado in 1706 and 1714, Du Tisne's in the southeast in 1719, Bourgmont's from the northeast half-way across Kansas to the Comanche country in 1724, and the Mallets' across the northwest en route to Santa Fe in 1739. The fleur-de-lis of France had been unfurled by the grand chiefs over at least three principal Indian nations of the area: the Kansa, the Wichita (Jumanos), and the Comanche. Bourgmont's efforts had effected a major treaty with the last named tribe allowing free access by French traders across Kansas and on to Santa Fe, and this privilege was actively pursued by the traders. Thus, the fort can be placed in context as a control point astride a well-developed trade route characterized, for the most part, by mutual trust and advantage on the part of French and Indians alike.

At least one woman was at the fort, probably the wife of a soldier or trader, as was Commandant La Barre's wife, and there were possibly others, since the policy of the French was to encourage marriages and settlement. Indeed, the post on the

Missouri was twice even raised to the dignity of *Colonie*, once in Deruisseau's license, and again in a dispatch from Macarty to Governor Vaudreuil on March 27, 1752. With soldiers, traders, workers, wives, horses, cows, boats, gardens, and tobacco and corn fields, it was at least well on the way to deserving the name.

Although the troops in the garrisons in upper Louisiana were a rather sorry-looking lot, the officers were well uniformed and wore their bright coats, embroidered vests, and knee breeches while going about their duties. We can assume that Cavagnial's walls were also witness to such pomp as could be mustered by commandants Villiers, La Barre, Portneuf, Moncharvaux, and their successor or successors.

The bateau convoy up from Kaskaskia or Chartres one or two times a year must have been a big occasion. At a small post like Cavagnial, the government convoy was probably combined with that of the private traders who, under Vaudreuil's license, were responsible for supplying the post and for transporting the troops. The fort was virtually isolated during the wintertime, since there was little overland travel and the river "highway" was frequently blocked with ice. Official correspondence came to a standstill until spring. But activity was at a high level at the fort during the winter, for that was the fur season. *Voyageurs* shipped in their trade goods in the summer and fall, traded them at the fort (and at outlying "little forts") for furs during the winter fur season, and sent the furs downriver in the spring. The traders' store at the post in the fur season must surely have been a lively place.

No definite records exist of men of the cloth at Cavagnial, but they probably were there at some time or times during its 20 years of existence. Father Mercier, the post missionary at Fort Orleans, went far across Kansas with Bourgmont and upon returning to the fort, chanted the first "Te Deum" on the Missouri on November 5, 1724. The Kansa always spoke reverently of the "black robes" (i.e., Jesuits). The following report appears in the 1727 dispatches from Canada:

20th October 1727 Mssrs. de Beauharnois and Dubois explanatory of two petitions of the Jesuit Fathers. Note—the Jesuits have, in the estimate of expenses, yearly: for the support of a Missionary at the Kanzas 600 li.

In April of 1734 Governor Bienville wrote to the minister of colonies that "the (seminary) priests of Cahokia have the Missoury where there are nations sufficiently numerous among whom they can exercise their zeal. . . ." Some day we may learn something of their successors, if any, at Fort de Cavagnial.

Probably the most picturesque account which could be given of the fort and its daily routine, somewhat overdrawn, was written near the turn of the century in the *History of the Kansa or Kaw Indians,* by G. P. Morehouse:

It was Kanses, an outpost of the progressive French, and one of their frontier towns, where white men lived in houses and carried on business almost 200 years ago. Here was a depot for all the commercial supplies of that day, the merchandise from distant France and the valuable skins and furs which were here stored for sale and exchange. . . . It was Kanses, an important French military post and fort, with its strong garrison of brave soldiers, one of that wonderful chain of French defenses established from Quebec to New Orleans and along the Missouri River. It was here that the stirring morning drum-beat and the solemn echo of the evening gun marked the first permanent establishment of white man's authority, protection and enterprise.

While one seldom gives it much thought, some of the greatest "Fathers of our Country"—our Midwestern country— were French. The Midwest has a long and illustrious colonial history. Consider, for example, that Fort de Cavagnial was founded, existed for two decades, and was abandoned long before the first California mission was established by Fray Junipero Serra at San Diego in 1769. Yet it is largely ignored, at the cost of some resulting historical drabness, because that

history was made by "foreigners," and its records are in many
cases still wrapped in an alien tongue. These dynamic people
explored and charted this wilderness, discovered, and named
the major rivers, mountains, and Indian tribes, tempered the
ferocity of the savages and made them dependent on trade
goods and hence amenable to civilized control, and established
some of the oldest settlements and churches in the Mississippi
and Missouri valleys. These French-Canadian explorers were
of a stock well-suited for such work, for they were almost all
Normans, descendants of the Vikings who settled in the
northwest of France. They were in a very real sense the first
pathfinders of the West, and they served as competent scouts
and interpreters for the advance parties of English-speaking
peoples who came after them. They deserve more recognition
than they have received.

So far as can be ascertained, the first commandant of Fort de
Cavagnial was the Chevalier François Coulon de Villiers, one
of six sons of Nicolas-Antoine Coulon de Villiers, nearly all of
whom figured prominently in the military service of New
France. His mother's sister was the famed Canadian heroine,
Madeleine de Vercheres, who, as a young girl, organized her
panic-stricken townsmen for a successful defense against an
Iroquois attack. Villiers was born in about 1712 in Vercheres,
France, served as a cadet in Canada (with his father and
brothers at Forts La Baye and St. Joseph), and was promoted
to ensign in 1736 (in Louisiana) and to lieutenant on June 1,
1746. He was in the Missouri country as early as 1742 and may
have been on hand at the start of construction of the fort in
1744. The promotion to lieutenant in 1746 probably was in
recognition of his status as commandant of Fort de Cavagnial,
the same rank or higher being accorded all four known
commandants there. Nothing is known of his service at the
Missouri post other than the fact that the troop lists show that
he commanded there. Bertet, the commander at the Illinois,
praised his intelligence and good conduct, and Vaudreuil
wrote a glowing account to the Minister Maurepas in Paris in

1747 regarding the effectiveness of the fort in curing the abuses leading to its establishment. Villiers probably served until near the expiration of Deruisseau's license.

In mid-1749 he participated in Celeron's famous tour through the upper Ohio region, involving the burying of leaden plates asserting France's right to that area. He thereafter commanded the Illinois convoy (i.e., the periodic movements of personnel and supplies on the Mississippi and adjacent rivers in armed bateaux) and directed successful sorties against the English forts to the east. On one of these expeditions in 1756, he recruited Indians at a war feast given by the great chief of the Illinois, saying that he was going "to avenge the death of his brother, Monsieur de Jumonville." The significance of this declaration will become apparent in the next paragraph. He was appointed aide-major (second in command) at Fort Chartres on November 28, 1757. At some time during this period he married the half sister of St. Ange, who was the last commandant at Fort de Chartres. St. Ange, who never married, left his estate to the Villiers children. Villiers also participated in the defeat of British General Grant in the eastern campaigns in 1758. In 1759 he, together with De Ligneris, Vaudreuil's old commander in the Fox campaign, was taken prisoner at Fort Niagara. Villiers served as second in command of the French relief force which was recruited in the west, and which suffered a decisive defeat at the battle of La Belle Famille, within sight of Fort Niagara. He was awarded the Cross of St. Louis in the same year. His death occurred May 22, 1794, at New Orleans.

An interesting historical sidelight regarding Villiers is the fact that his brother, Jumonville, was the French officer who was fired upon and killed by young Col. George Washington's men near Fort Duquesne in present western Pennsylvania in 1754. Another brother, Louis Villiers, who was at Fort Duquesne, instantly set out with a detachment of troops to avenge his brother's death, surrounded Washington's men at Fort Necessity, and forced his capitulation. It is to the Villiers' credit that Louis, in spite of the claimed "assassination" of his brother, allowed Washington to go free—and thus on to the wider stage of American history.

The story of the next commandant at Fort Cavagnial is a tragic vignette. Augustin-Antoine de la Barre, Seigneur de Jardin, was a promising young officer who had the good fortune of marrying Marie-Anne Adhemar de Lantagnac on November 28, 1741, in Quebec. Honore Bouche, a seventeenth-century historian, traced the history of the Adhemars back to the seventh century Lambert Adhemar de Monteil. As leaders in the Crusades, the Adhemars were commemorated in history and in the verse of Tasso. (The daughter of Madame de Sevigne, that celebrated lady of letters during Louis XIV's reign, married into the Adhemar family.) La Barre's wife was the older Governor Vaudreuil's grandniece (and second cousin of the then Governor Vaudreuil of Louisiana). He may have been related to Gov. Antoine LeFebvre La Barre who succeeded Frontenac. La Barre had been an ensign in Canada and Louisiana and was promoted to lieutenant on June 11, 1750, contemporaneously with the commandantship of Fort de Cavagnial. There is no doubt that he was the protegé of Vaudreuil, who thus assigned his young cousin's husband to what was considered a very lucrative post in which he could make his fortune if all went well. But all did not go well. For on February 24, 1751, he was murdered by a soldier at Fort de Cavagnial who was drunk on brandy sold to him, against the Illinois commandant's instructions, by two Canadian *voyageurs.* The culprit was tried before a council of war and shot on March 18, 1751. Both *voyageurs* were imprisoned. Vaudreuil, La Jonquiere (the then governor of New France), and Celeron (commandant at Detroit) took note of the matter in their reports, and Celeron noted what a "good officer" La Barre had been. Michel, Intendant of Louisiana, in a long letter to the Minister of Marine told of La Barre's assassination. His own account cannot be improved upon for drama and human interest:

We learn from the Arkansas savages that M. de la Barre, another relative of de Vaudreuil on his side as well as on his wife's side, and Commander in the Missouri, has just been killed with a gun shot *(coup de fusil)* by a soldier of his little garrison, who in deserting took the wife of this officer. This news merits confirmation but it was, however, well-detailed by these savages and the people who know them think that they are telling the truth. There, Monsieur is the fruit of the discipline in this country. Neither officer nor soldier—nobody knows it. One blames it all on the soldier since he drank all his money at the canteen where they give them drugs which ruin their health.

What consternation this must have caused when the news reached Paris and word got around of this calamity, with scandalous overtones, which had befallen the great family Adhemar de Lantagnac! Even more interesting to us, outweighing, perhaps, our momentary sympathy for her unfortunate husband, is the fact that Marie-Anne Adhemar de Lantagnac, of one of the first families of France, was the *first European woman* definitely known to have lived in Kansas. Scandal, one is relieved to say, can apparently be eliminated, and at worst the episode seems to have been merely an abduction. Madame La Barre never remarried, so far as we know, and she was for years a respected resident at Kaskaskia, even being consulted in governmental matters. Her touching handwritten letter to Governor Vaudreuil mourning the death of "Monsieur La Barre" (still preserved in the Loudon Collection) takes on considerably more significance now that we know her importance in Kansas history. The text of her letter is set out below:

Monsieur:

I have received, with all possible satisfaction, the letters which you had written to me. It is the goodness of heart with which you take an interest in the re-establishment of my health. Since the death of Monsieur La Barre, I am unable to enjoy perfect health myself. I have the very grievous situation in which I see myself reduced without hope to pull myself out of it until I might be in a position to leave the country. I am unable to express to you the crosses which I bear every day. I do not receive any consolation until I receive your loving news, which will always be for me a new obligation to you. I flatter myself that you would indeed not wish to refuse the person who has the honor of sending her respects, Monsieur.

Your very humble and very obedient servant,
Lantagnac de la Barre, Widow

Her sons were placed in the troops and not rotated, so as to be able to remain with her at Kaskaskia. Upon learning of Vaudreuil's appointment as governor-general, she decided to move to Canada and apparently made the trip via Pimitou (Peoria) and Mackinac in the spring of 1753.

La Barre's successor at Cavagnial was Louis Robineau de Portneuf, surely one of the most energetic and versatile junior officers in Louisiana. With him the recorded history of the fort reaches full flood. He became an ensign *en pied* on October 1, 1740, and on August 6, 1741, married Marie Therese Trudeau, widow of Alphonse de la Buissonniere, a former commandant at the Illinois.

Portneuf's wife merits comment. Her marriage to La Buissonniere had been strenuously opposed by officials and clergy, since as a commoner she was below the station of her fiancé, an officer. So the intrepid couple eloped to Spanish Pensacola (Florida) and were wed there. Returning to the Illinois, and a storm of protest, the bride caught smallpox at Natchez, returned to her father's home, and was finally, after two long years, reunited with her husband at the Illinois by a special dispensation at court obtained by Governor Bienville. Then, to crown romance with tragedy, La Buissonniere died suddenly of apoplexy not long thereafter, on December 11, 1740. Apparently, as an officer's widow, she did not encounter the same problems in marrying Portneuf. The minutes of the March 5, 1746, session of the superior council of Louisiana (at New Orleans) contain an interesting report of a suit brought against Portneuf by a cousin of La Buissonniere, claiming to be his sole heir and creditor, and also a report of an action brought by Portneuf regarding the property of a minor relative of his wife's for whom she had been acting as tutor (guardian).

Regarding Portneuf, the writer Bossu wrote that he had formerly commanded at Fort Orleans. He is on record as searching for lead and copper mines in 1743 in the Illinois region, carrying out the policy of Bertet, the commandant at Fort de Chartres. In 1747 Bertet, commandant of the Illinois, sent him on a reconnaissance expedition to the Wabash to feel out their loyalty, lately swayed by the English, and to incite attacks by them on the English settlements near Philadelphia. This seems to have been an assignment for which he had special talents, since he went on a number of such expeditions. He was apparently second in command at Chartres for a time, and went from that post to the Missouri in 1751, having meanwhile been commissioned a lieutenant on June 11, 1750.

At the time Portneuf took command at Fort Cavagnial, matters were going well for France in *Haute Louisiane*. Bertet, his superior, at the Illinois, had been an unusually capable officer. Vaudreuil issued to Bertet's successor, Macarty, on August 8, 1751, a very detailed and well planned "Order of Command" for the government of the Illinois country. In it he dealt with all manner of things for the supposed good of the infant colony; for example, he opposed the engagement by the habitants of attorneys, "whose subtleties would become of dangerous consequence." He referred to the garrisons subject to the Illinois command: Kaskaskia, Fort de Chartres, Vincennes, "the Missouri" (i.e., Fort de Cavagnial) and Cahokia, of which he noted that the posts at the Missouri and at Cahokia were the smaller. He cautioned against the excesses of the Canadian traders and noted that the Missouri post should be supported by the *voyageurs* and that its trade would be "very lucrative" to its commanding officer.

Portneuf was at his new post by September 9, 1751, for on that date Vaudreuil wrote the first of several dispatches to Macarty insisting that Portneuf, the Missouri commandant, pay a sizable obligation to one M. Olivier. In his reply (in January, 1752) Macarty called attention to the difficulties of communication with the Missouri post and stated that he would have to forward Vaudreuil's order in the spring. He mentioned two traders, the Sieurs Despins and Larche, who intended to go to the Indians in the vicinity of Portneuf's post in the spring. He also noted the difficulties of carrying out the usual troop rotations at the remote Missouri post and ended with a plea for orders assuring the usual "gratification" from the traders to Portneuf, whom he was leaving at the Missouri. Sometime in 1752 the Indians, according to Bossu, gave "Baron de Portneuf" a fine soft fur "spotted with black and pearly white" from an unknown animal "twice as big as a European fox," which he sent to Madame Vaudreuil, who had it made into a muff.

In the meantime, Portneuf and Fort de Cavagnial were playing a part in one of the most interesting events of the French occupation in the West. The quasi-official Chapuis expedition to Santa Fe spent the winter of 1751-1752 at Cavagnial, surely the high point of its history. Counting the ten men in the expedition, the ten soldiers of the garrison, the commandant and an interpreter, the several post traders and their employees, possibly a few French wives (plus some Indian common-law wives), and French and French-Kansa children, there must have been nearly 50 souls in or near Fort de Cavagnial all that winter. Since they were still there by Mardi Gras, one can imagine that it was celebrated with gusto by the entire assemblage, as was the custom in both upper and lower Louisiana.

The two leaders of the expedition were Jean Chapuis and Louis Feuilli. The latter had been an interpreter in the King's service for eight years among the Osage, Missouri, and Kansa.

The others were Roy, Jean Dron, Aubuchon, Calve, Luis Trudeau, Lorenzo Trudeau, Betille, and du Charme. Chapuis and Feuilli had purchased a sizable amount of cloth goods, tools, and other trade goods at Mackinac in July, 1751, from an individual named Clicancourt and from the firm of Landevil le Fer and Company. They obtained the usual trading permit from the commandant at Mackinac and set out for the Illinois. There, they laid before the ad interim commandant at Fort de Chartres, Benoist de St. Claire, their plans to open large scale trade with Santa Fe. Whether their plan was actually initiated by the French government is not known, but once arrived at Chartres, their expedition was given official sanction. St. Claire wrote out a formal permit on October 6, 1751, allowing them to carry their trade goods to New Mexico and permitting Chapuis to carry the French flag, a badge of authority generally reserved for the "troupes de la marine" and leading chiefs of the friendly tribes. He also ordered them to protect each other and to stay together until they reached New Mexico, an injunction which eight of them flatly ignored when the going got rough.

With winter fast approaching, they probably set out without much further delay up the Missouri for Fort de Cavagnial. Portneuf was there at the time. Since, as will be recalled, one of the principal missions of the Missouri post was to penetrate to Santa Fe in order to discover the route and "establish trade easily with the Spaniards," it can be assumed that he gave the expedition all possible assistance. Feuilli later stated affirmatively that the Missouri commandant added his permission to that of St. Claire's.

While at Cavagnial, Chapuis and Feuilli executed several legal papers, the full texts of which are still extant, including a contract briefly outlining the undertaking and reciting a promise by Chapuis to provide certain trade goods to Feuilli, and a promissory note from Feuilli to Chapuis, or his order (payable in beaver skins!) in consideration therefor. These instruments, dated December 9, 1751, and a letter, apparently to Chapuis, dated two days earlier, all recite on their face that they were written at "Fort Cavagnial." So far as the writer can determine, these papers have the distinction of being the first known legal instruments executed in Kansas.

The party left Cavagnial on about March 23, 1752. Their route was first by bateaux up the Missouri and westward via the Platte, and then overland the remainder of the trip. In addition to whatever personal mounts they had for the overland leg, we know they had nine horses loaded with their trade goods. All but Chapuis and Feuilli deserted the expedition at the Pawnee country, since they lacked the fortitude to press on. The remaining two proceeded ahead toward Santa Fe, having fortunately befriended an A'e Indian woman who knew the route. At the Rio Ganillos some Apaches, friendly to the Spaniards, met them and conducted them to the pueblo of Pecos on August 6, 1752, where a rude shock awaited them.

For in their haste to establish profitable trade with Santa Fe, they had failed to ascertain the attitude of the governor, Velez. Furious over the release of the Mallets and later traders, he had made it clear that the practice was not to be tolerated. The two Frenchmen were therefore promptly taken into custody by the missionary at Pecos, Father Juan Joseph Toledo, and were conducted from thence to Santa Fe by the alcalde, mayor of Pecos and Galisteo, Don Thomas de Sena. There their goods were sold at auction to pay the expenses of their prison confinement, and they were thoroughly interrogated by the governor and sent on to Mexico for more questioning. They were eventually put on board ship and sent to Spain (Cadiz) where they were imprisoned. The full transcripts of their interrogations are preserved, along with the texts of all their papers and the inventory of their goods. Among their papers was found a letter from Feuilli addressed to "Monsieur Moreau" (who married and lived on in Santa Fe after arriving with the Mallets) requesting his aid with the Spanish governor. Apparently it was never delivered. All of their papers and depositions, together with a complete mémoire on the entire affair (and all preceding French intrusions into New Mexico) were sent by the Council of the Indies to the Spanish King at Madrid.

The council viewed the matter as an extremely serious one, and the two traders narrowly escaped the death penalty. The Spanish fiscal in Madrid was absolutely certain that the expedition was an official reconnaissance sponsored by the French government and cast in the guise of a private trading expedition. The prisoners' persistent requests, while in New Spain, to be allowed to return in order to report to the Illinois commandant did not help to dispel this view. It is apparent from the depositions that Chapuis carefully avoided mentioning Fort de Cavagnial, but the younger Feuilli was a little easier to "brainwash" and hence the existence of the fort, the size of its garrison, and its proximity to the New Mexican dependencies was brought forcibly to the attention of the Spanish King. The Spanish translation (rendered in English) of Feuilli's description of Cavagnial is rather quaint: "In this pueblo there is a detachment of ten soldiers and a lieutenant of the presidio of Illinois."

Cavagnial had already been brought to the attention of the Spaniards in New Mexico, however, probably for the first time, in 1749, by one Satren, a Frenchman. He had gone with two others to the Taos fair and was taken into custody and required to give a deposition, wherein he told of the existence of the fort.

Of Chapuis and Feuilli, two of the truly original trailblazers to Santa Fe, nothing further is known. Let us take leave of them by noting their rather prophetic description to the New Mexican authorities of a potential Santa Fe trade wherein "clothing and effects could be transported to Santa Fe in caravans of horses" which caravans would each need to be escorted by "fifty or sixty armed men" in order to guard against "the Pawnees and the Comanches." This is exactly what did transpire—nearly three-quarters of a century later.

Returning to Fort de Cavagnial, we find that in the spring of

1752 Portneuf was again assigned the task of stirring up war parties of the Indians, in this case the Missouri. He also complained that the Kansa had moved away from the fort, so that he no longer saw the *voyageurs* in the wintertime. This was doubly unfortunate for him, since he could not carry out his mission to control them, nor could he demand his "gratification." He sent three of his men to Kaskaskia for provisions and to relay his complaint against one Avion, a trader, who had settled some distance below Cavagnial on the Kansas River, enticed the Kansa away, and then laughed at Portneuf's demands to desist. (This free-enterprising gentleman seems to have the distinction of being the first entrepreneur having a location of any degree of permanence in or near the present Kansas City metropolitan area.) Portneuf also renewed his plea for authority to levy the customary gratification on the traders and to force them to trade at the fort. He stated that even the Indians urged this control "to avoid the uproar of the voyageurs who snatch a beaver pelt from each other." Regarding the fort itself, then nearly eight years old, he pointed out that both the fort and the barracks were all rotten and that they needed rebuilding. He also suggested that due to the removal of the Indians, it might be necessary to relocate the fort southward (near present Kansas City).

Vaudreuil, meanwhile, was delighted with Macarty's choice of Portneuf for permanent commander of Cavagnial and wrote noting his abilities in dealing with the tribes and confirming his gratification and control over the traders, adding that the King should bear none of the expense of this post.

Portneuf apparently arrived at Kaskaskia himself near the end of April, 1752, leaving for Fort de Cavagnial again on July 4. While at Kaskaskia, he was again assigned the task of getting the Missouri and Osage to send out war parties against unfriendly tribes. Since the Kansa had by this time returned to their village in the vicinity of the fort, he was directed to rebuild it. There had been a flurry of activity at Cavagnial while its commandant was away. The corporal whom he had left in charge there reported to Macarty that after Portneuf left for Kaskaskia an incident occurred which involved the wounding of a woman, either French or half-breed since an Indian would have customarily been described as such in the reports, and the killing of a cow. Also, the Missouri Indians had come on a horse-stealing foray to the fort and two of them were killed by the garrison, the only shots "fired in anger" from the fort so far as is known. To top it all they had had a violent windstorm which did damage to all the buildings and left not a chimney standing. Incidentally, the presence of cows and horses at Cavagnial was confirmed years later by a Frenchman in Lewis and Clark's party who said that when the French occupied the fort at the Kansa, they kept their cows and horses on the islands (probably Kickapoo and Cow islands) in the Missouri River.

Near the end of 1752, Portneuf reported to Macarty that the Spaniards had been trying to get the Iatan to guide them to the Missouri's area, to which they said they had penetrated previously. Macarty had arranged to have the two years' arrears in Portneuf's gratification paid by the *voyageurs* and at long last was able to satisfy therefrom the Missouri commandant's obligation to Monsieur Olivier. Portneuf also reported that he feared for two traders who had apparently been killed by the Little Osage. Macarty ordered him, as well as the *voyageurs,* to set about to discover a mine (to no avail as far as we know), and also ordered him to have the *voyageurs* pay for the repairs to the fort.

In 1753, four of Portneuf's men deserted but were later killed by the Wichita Indians. Also, in the same year it was reported that the Spaniards had sent troop convoys to the Pawnee country, some going to the area where the Villasur massacre had occurred, only a few days' travel from Fort de Cavagnial. One can imagine that the garrison was very much on the *qui-vive* during this period of increased Spanish activity. Macarty, the Illinois commandant, anticipating by a half-century the discoveries of Lewis and Clark, wrote in the same year of the Missouri River that "it is claimed that by that river you can reach the Sea of the West [i.e., the Pacific], passing the crest of the mountains [i.e., Rockies] on which you can find a river [i.e., the Columbia] which falls into that part of the Sea."

In the fall of 1753, Portneuf was recalled to the Illinois in order to go on what proved to be a futile provision supply expedition ordered by Governor Duquesne and Intendant Bigot of Canada. The Sieur de Marin, with 3,000 men, was making a tour de force through the northeastern border country to discourage the English, establish forts on the Ohio, and awe the fickle Indians into submission. This major military expedition was the first step which led up to the French-English clashes preceding the Seven Years' War. The Sieur des Mazellieres, a captain, with Portneuf, another lieutenant, and three ensigns were put in charge of a hundred-man supply expedition ordered up from the Illinois by the Canadian officials to meet Marin at a none-too-definite rendezvous point. The two groups never met. Low water on the rivers held up the progress of the main army, and Portneuf, due to an incompetent guide, managed to become lost for four days while out on patrol trying to make contact. Then hostile Shawnees made him beat a hasty retreat. Mazellieres was forced to make an enormous cache of the entire supply of provisions for the winter. The main supply force straggled back to the Illinois in November, and Portneuf arrived soon after. To Portneuf's credit, Kerlerec, the new governor of Louisiana, was able to report in June, 1754, that Portneuf had retraced his footsteps, successfully located the cache, and reported it to be well preserved.

That Portneuf was a man of some vision, who might himself have become one of the pathfinders of the West, is evident from the following account related by Bossu:

In 1754, Baron de Portneuf told me about his plan to explore the western part of Louisiana, by going up the

Mississippi and the Missouri, whose sources are unknown to us. This Canadian officer has the necessary qualifications for such enterprise, but the war which has broken out between England and France over their territorial boundaries on this continent has prevented him from carrying out his plan. I can assure you that I would have been very happy to accompany him. . . .

Bossu himself deserves a brief special mention. He has been referred to several times in this book. Here was an alert, intelligent, and highly candid young French officer who toured much of the Illinois country during the very period we are considering. He provides an articulate, eyewitness account of people and events which figure prominently in this narrative. He was personally acquainted with and wrote brief, but telling, comments about King Louis XV, Maurepas, Vaudreuil, Macarty, François Villiers, Portneuf, Moncharvaux, and many others, including the ubiquitous and ever interesting Indians. His chatty letters, assembled in book form, cast an aura of everyday human reality about what might otherwise seem a dry recitation of long past events.

Somewhat more is known of Portneuf. It is not certain that he ever returned to Cavagnial, although he may have. We do know that he was made a captain on July 1, 1759. There are ample records attesting that he was at the Upper Ohio as commandant of the important portage of Fort Presqu'isle from March, 1757 until 1759. Portneuf was nominal commandant of the entire Ohio region when De Ligneris evacuated in the summer of 1759 to escape the English. He carried on a spirited exchange of notes with the English regarding the terms of a possible surrender of his fort, most of these records being still preserved in copy form. Portneuf is last heard of in Detroit on October 13, 1759, and that garrison surrendered to the British six weeks later.

The year 1755 was notable for the fact that a number of the braves of the Kansa village (which was situated near, and was under the jurisdiction of, Fort de Cavagnial) participated in the final stages of the celebrated defeat of British Gen. Edward Braddock. Braddock was commander in chief and had arrived with his official staff and two regiments of troops in February of that year. His objective was Fort Duquesne, in present western Pennsylvania, which only the year before had been the subject of the skirmishes involving two of the Villiers brothers and George Washington, as noted previously. He took so long in reaching his objective that the French had time to marshal their forces, including a large number of Indians. Macarty, the Illinois commandant stationed at the newly rebuilt Fort de Chartres, recruited a sizable body of Little Osage and Kansa, probably with the assistance of the commandant at Cavagnial. Macarty furnished the Indians with powder and ball, and their rendezvous with the main French body took place at or near Fort Niagara. The Kansa contingent arrived just after the fight had ended.

It is not beyond the realm of possibility, however, that these recruits from Fort de Cavagnial may have sent a ball or two in the direction of the future father of our country. Young George Washington, at the head of the Virginia militia, took charge of the British forces after Braddock was mortally wounded and was very much in evidence in fighting the rear guard action which held off the pursuing Indians and saved the British from utter annihilation. A young wagoner in that fray may also have ducked a Kansa ball. His name was Daniel Boone, and some of his descendants later settled near Kansa territory. The Kansa and Little Osage suffered terrible hardships on their return to the Missouri River country, being en route seven months (well into the next winter season) and were forced to eat their horses along the way in order to stay alive. This fascinating tale was related years later to Lt. Zebulon Pike by Chtoka, or Wet Stone, a Little Osage, when Pike visited that tribe in 1806. Pike also stopped at the village of the Osage Chief Pawhuska, who had been the ranking chief of the Osage, Kansa, and Otoe at Braddock's defeat. Pawhuska, then grown old, took Pike to his lodge and showed him a scarlet coat and a blond scalp he had taken on that fateful date in 1755.

In 1756, the Seven Years' War began in Europe and its equivalent, the French and Indian War, began (or rather continued) in America. It had actually started two years before with the skirmishes of the colonials over Fort Duquesne.

Bougainville, Montcalm's aide-de-camp, mentioned Fort Cavagnial in 1757 in a status of forces report. He noted that at the village of the "Kanze" the French had "a garrison with a commandant appointed, as is the case with Peoria and Fort Chartres, by New Orleans." He also reported that the post produced annually a hundred bundles of furs, including a great many beavers that were badly worked.

The fort was apparently commanded at that time by Captain de Moncharvaux. A cadet soldier, probably his second in command, and four gunners also appear in the troop lists as serving at the Missouri at that time. Moncharvaux's full name was Jean François Tisserant de Moncharvaux (or Montchervaux). He was an ensign in 1732, promoted to lieutenant in 1736 and to captain in 1747. He married in 1721 and had four sons baptized in the period from 1724 to 1729. The dispatches refer to his "numerous family." He had one brush with scandal which he successfully lived down. Put in charge of the Illinois convoy in 1749, he was accused of pilfering the King's liquor, drinking with the troops and habitants, and breaking open the King's military stores to pay his debts along the route. Both Governor Vaudreuil and Intendant Michel in letters to Versailles said he should be pardoned, Michel adding that he had done no more (and probably less) than was customary. Vaudreuil called him a "good officer," and Michel said he had "served usefully during several wars, being known and loved by all the Indians." In early December, 1751, while on garrison duty in the Kaskaskia area, his company, under his personal leadership, quelled an incipient uprising among the Illinois tribes. Bossu participated in the planning and execution of this operation and wrote glowingly of Moncharvaux's part therein, calling him an "intelligent and brave officer" and praising his "vigilance." One of Madame La Barre's sons served in Moncharvaux's company in 1752 after the elder La Barre was killed at Cavagnial.

On July 18, 1754, Governor Kerlerec (who replaced Vaudreuil in Louisiana) addressed a petition to the Minister of Colonies in behalf of "M. Moncharvaux, Captain commander at the Post of Missouri." He enclosed the captain's own letter request, noting that he was a "very bad orator," but adding that "he is encumbered with a very large family and this would be a very great charity for you to help him in the favor which he asks." The letter of Moncharvaux is apparently not extant, but notes on Kerlerec's mémoire seem to indicate that the request was directed to a French abbot—perhaps regarding the education of a son or daughter in his "large family." Earlier, Vaudreuil in his letter of March 15, 1747, to Maurepas had noted that Moncharvaux was then commanding at the Arkansas post. Regarding him, the governor noted that he had "only the best references." He noted that he had directed Moncharvaux to treat with the Arkansas and "pay them [for] the hairs gracefully"—apparently a term of the trade meaning to deal with them diplomatically when trading for their furs. Moncharvaux was still in the Illinois country (possibly at Cavagnial) as late as 1758, but after that time there seems to be no more mention of him.

The fort was listed by name in an official report the next year, when Governor Kerlerec of Louisiana on December 12, 1758, reported on the friendly tribes and French installations in their areas. He noted that "Fort Cavagnolle" consisted of a "circle of piles" enclosing "some bad cabins and huts." He reported further that the garrison there consisted of an officer and seven or eight soldiers, plus a number of traders. He also noted that the Kansa had been reduced by smallpox (and Pawnee wars) to not over three hundred braves and that they were "very attached to the French."

It is interesting to speculate on how the fort was reduced from a square stockade with bastioned corners and stout buildings within to a circle of piles enclosing bad cabins and crude huts. The apparent reason is fairly obvious. Portneuf in 1752 was, it will be recalled, left virtually to his own devices by the higher command. Though he pleaded to Macarty for money and for instructions regarding repairs to the badly run-down fort, the answers were slow in coming, and when they did, he was simply told to collect his own gratification from the traders and to see that they repaired the fort at no expense to the King. Thrown on his own resources, yet responsible for the defensive integrity of the fort, he may have economized on both time and material by tearing down the old bastions and stockade and rebuilding the stockade in a circle surrounding the existing buildings, using the salvageable older timbers and such new ones as were necessary. As to the buildings themselves, it is known that they were badly damaged and their chimneys all blown down in the 1752 windstorm, and they, too, were probably never put back to their original condition and were apparently allowed to depreciate badly thereafter.

New France's star was fast falling in 1759, for Wolfe's men stormed the Plains of Abraham and took Quebec in spite of Montcalm's valiant defense. The next year, Governor-General Vaudreuil-Cavagnial—the namesake of Fort Cavagnial—surrendered Montreal to the British. All Canada was lost.

A fitting note upon this era was struck by the beleaguered Aubry, the last French national to act as Governor of Louisiana. He bemoaned the "stretched-out country which with its different nations is so full and difficult to govern" and added that he had, regretfully, presided over "the transfer of a half to England and the other to Spain." He concluded "my position is most unusual. I command for the King of France and at the same time I govern the colony as if it belonged to the King of Spain—a French commander [and] French form with Spanish derivation." It was the twilight of France in America.

But surprisingly enough, life went on very nearly as usual in the Illinois and Missouri country. In spite of the nominal transfer of New Orleans and the trans-Mississippi region (including Fort de Cavagnial) to Spain and of the French area east of the Mississippi to England by the Treaty of Paris in 1763, neither power occupied its newly acquired territory for a few years. Pontiac's war stopped the English while lack of funds, manpower, and interest stopped the Spanish. Thus, the post on the Missouri could be described in 1763 as being still garrisoned "by the detachment from the Illinois" and a "great commerce in furs was carried on" with the Indians there. D'Abbadie, the newly appointed French director-general of Louisiana, arrived on June 29, 1763, with power granted by the King to "suppress or maintain distant posts" (indicating indirectly that there were still such distant posts). Interestingly enough, the news of the cession of his new jurisdiction to Spain was not reported to D'Abbadie until after he arrived in Louisiana.

One of the last official references to the period of operation of Fort de Cavagnial was recorded on May 22, 1764, when the French official, Vilemont, (under Spanish control) wrote the first of three mémoires to Grimaldi, Minister of War and Marine at Madrid, urging the Spanish to follow the French example and keep a post among the tribes of the Missouri. He referred to the "existing entrepôt" (i.e., the trading post at Cavagnial) and urged that it be strengthened and better provided with merchandise.

The final comment on the French garrison which was still at Fort de Cavagnial comes from Auguste Chouteau. In 1763, he had gone with Pierre Laclede upriver from Chartres to select a site for the new trading post of Maxent, Laclede and Company—the genesis of St. Louis, Missouri. Years later, writing in his journal from personal knowledge, he noted that in 1764 Neyon de Villiers (not one of the six famous brothers), commandant at the Illinois, acting on the orders of Governor D'Abbadie, "brought down the little garrison" of the "Fort des

Canses" as well as all the other garrisons from the evacuated
French forts. He added that all of the troops were collected at
Fort de Chartres, and the bulk of them went downriver to New
Orleans under Villiers on July 10, 1764, leaving a garrison of
40 men under St. Ange to deliver Chartres to the British. (St.
Ange, incidentally, had been Bourgmont's second in command on the expedition into Kansas, thereafter commanding
at Fort Orleans and Fort Vincennes.) It is known from other
sources that the date of the general order from Governor
D'Abbadie to evacuate all of the French posts in upper
Louisiana was January 30, 1764. The first traders' convoy in
the spring of that year probably carried the order to the
garrison.

Fort de Chartres, and with it all French jurisdiction in upper
Louisiana, was surrendered to Lieutenant Stirling and his
Black Watch regiment by Commandant St. Ange and Commissary Deruisseau on October 10, 1765. The heritage of Fort
de Cavagnial lived on only in the French names of many of the
Kansa, and a vague tribal memory of their connection with the
fort which flew the ensign of the lilies of France.

There is an interesting and tantalizing sequel to the story.
Before Cavagnial is dismissed as a charming historical will-o'-
the wisp whose parade-ground men shall never tread again,
the following should be considered: On July 2, 1804, Lewis
and Clark (with the aid of a French-speaking guide and
French maps) camped opposite the old Kansa village, just
above Kickapoo Island. Having heard of the fort, they crossed
the river and searched for it. About a mile inland from the site
of the former Indian village and on "rising ground," they
found the location of the fort, which was clearly identifiable
due to the "remains of chimneys and the general outlines of the
fortification, as well as by the fine spring which supplied it with
water." The spring flowed into a "Turkey Creek" (Plum
Creek?) which flowed around behind the village site and into
the Missouri.

Another famous western American expedition took note of

the site of Fort de Cavagnial. Dr. Edwin James, the surgeon, naturalist, and reporter for Maj. S. H. Long's expedition in 1819-1820, with part of Long's group, viewed the area in 1819. Dr. James wrote in his official journal that "the site of an old village of Kanzas, and the remains of a fortification erected by the French, were pointed out a few miles below Isle au Vache."

Still later—in 1833—Alexander Philip Maximilian, passing up the Missouri, near Independence Creek, observed "naked grassy eminences, where a village of Kanzas formerly stood. . . . The Spaniards [French] had a post of a few soldiers here."

Another singular coincidence regarding the site of the old fort can be pointed out. In the spring of 1846 young Francis Parkman, who wrote *The Oregon Trail*, visited the Kickapoo Indian settlement a few miles north of Fort Leavenworth. This was the same Parkman who in later years was the master historian of France in America, writing volume after volume which culminated in his matchless commentary on Montcalm and Wolfe at Quebec. Describing the village of the Kickapoos, Parkman, in *The Oregon Trail*, told of "a swift little stream, working its devious way down a woody valley." The coincidence is that this little stream was Plum Creek, and the Kickapoo village could not have been very far from the probable site of Fort de Cavagnial. Indeed, the spring of the fort may have flowed into the same stream. Thus, Parkman in all probability crossed at least the periphery of the site of the westernmost outpost of France in Upper Louisiana—and was totally unaware of the fact. Apparently by 1846 all trace of the fort had vanished, and none of those in Parkman's party or at the Indian village knew of its previous existence.

Where are the remains of Fort de Cavagnial today? Candor compels the confession that they have not yet been located. Those who have been interested in determining the site have, collectively speaking, flown over in a helicopter, studied aerial photographs, driven around and over it, dug trenches in every direction, and walked over practically every square foot of it—and have found no definite trace. The apparent general site has been visited (and in some cases preliminarily excavated) by representatives of the University of Kansas, Kansas State University, the University of Missouri, the National Park Service, the Smithsonian Institution, the Kansas Parks Department, and the Kansas State Historical Society.

Fort de Cavagnial was, for a brief time, the first "city of Kansas," i.e., the point of contact of European civilization with the Kansa tribe and the vast area bearing their name. As such it was the indirect predecessor of the community of the same name which was later platted on Gabriel Prudhomme's farm at Kawsmouth after the French-American François Chouteau set up his Kansa trading station there. For 20 years "Kansas" and "Missouri" meant Fort de Cavagnial—and Cavagnial was French.

CHAPTER IV

The Custom of Paris in Mid-America

FEW KANSAS CITIANS ARE AWARE that present metropolitan Kansas City and the entire Kansas and western Missouri area were subject to the colonial laws of France from 1682 to 1763 (and even later if we count the Spanish and American recognition and enforcement of French law, extending into the early 1800s). Fewer still are aware that the writ of Louis XIV and Louis XV could be and was enforced on the spot in this area by administrators, attorneys, judges, and troops operating out of Fort Kaskaskia and Fort de Chartres in the Illinois country during the entire early and middle 1700s, by the garrison at Fort Orleans in mid-Missouri in the 1720s, and from 1744 until 1764 by the *congé* and troops at Fort de Cavagnial just north of present Ft. Leavenworth, Kansas.

French law died hard in eastern Missouri. Some St. Louis attorneys made a living for years trying the "Spanish Titles" (many of which were really French titles from the early *Livre Terrein,* i.e., land book, in St. Louis). But in Kansas or western Missouri one must recognize that any discussion of the law of colonial France has principally an antiquarian interest now. It might have been otherwise. Had Fort Orleans or Fort de Cavagnial or the farming community below Wolf River (near Highland, Kansas, 1795-96) resulted in permanent settlements, they would doubtless have left for a time an appreciable legacy of French law on both sides of the Missouri River near them, just as did the settlements on the Mississippi in the Illinois country. In any event, it is interesting to know that a

89

legal system other than the English common law obtained for
such a long time in the Midwest, and in Kansas City. This
awareness may serve not only to edify us but perhaps also to
make us more appreciative of the ascendancy of our own
system of law.

This chapter is not intended to be a definitive study of the
law of metropolitan France in the seventeenth and eighteenth
centuries. Rather, it is a collection for laymen of those few
recorded instances when that law was in some way involved in
the backwoods, westernmost part of *Haute Louisiane*—a country
then as dangerous, new, and exciting as we now consider
Antarctica, or perhaps the moon. We must interpolate from
those few examples to get some idea of the system of French
colonial law which like an iceberg 90 percent lay beneath the
surface.

On the theory that a government is effective to the extent of
the geographical limits within which its writ will run, let us
begin by exploring the domains of colonial France in the New
World. The Sieur Du Tisne explored southeastern Kansas in
1719, raised the royal white flag with the fleur-de-lis at the
Pawnee village, and also erected a cross bearing the arms of
France. Both Spain and France almost built forts on the
Kansas River in 1722, which would have established a clear
frontier, but these two forts never materialized. The westernmost forts of the French were the redoubt built by Bourgmont
on Isle au Vache in the Missouri River near present Oak Mills,
Kansas (1714), Fort Orleans in present Carroll County,
Missouri (1723-1729), and Fort de Cavagnial (1744-1764). The
easternmost Spanish fort in this general area was El Quartelejo
in eastern Colorado. French control in the Kansas-Missouri
area became less theoretical and more factual after the turn of
the century. Indians from this area had, of course, been visiting
and trading furs at the Illinois posts since the late 1600s. In this
manner they were exposed in a way to the laws of the French,
since the fur trade was governed by these laws. As the French
pushed their search for furs westward and northward up the

Plaque commemorating Fort de Cavagnial, near Ft. Leavenworth.

Missouri River, they took their law with them. *Voyageurs* and coureurs de bois may have reached the Kansas River by the late 1690s and a more definitcly reported instance of such a trip, by Le Sueur, occurred in 1705. In all probability there were French fur traders on the Missouri as far as (or beyond) present Kansas City in every year from 1700 onward. The Sieur de Bourgmont, as we have seen, in 1723 established Fort Orleans on the Missouri River near present-day Brunswick, Missouri. Using the fort as a base, he formally established suzerainty over the Kansa, Pawnees, Otoes, and the Padoucas or Plains Comanches, far out on the plains of Kansas. The troops garrisoned at Forts Kaskaskia and Chartres, at Fort Orleans, and later at Fort Cavagnial (as well as the chiefs of the grand villages of the friendly tribes, the Missouri, the Kansa, the Pawnees, the Wichitas, and the Comanches, who proudly flew the royal white fleur-de-lis flag of *l'ancien régime* of France) provided that degree of force necessary to make the laws effective.

The form of government within which these laws were applied was an absolute monarchy under both Louis XIV and Louis XV. When Louis XIV said *"l'état, c'est moi"* (if he ever did), *l'etat* included the Missouri-Kansas area. The Minister of Colonies was next in authority below the King in overseas matters. Below him was a resident royal Governor of Louisiana appointed by the King. This colonial governor in turn appointed a commandant and commissaire ordonnateur for the Illinois, one of nine districts of the Colony of Louisiana. The lowest military, administrative, and legal positions on this plan of organization were held by the commandants in the several military posts scattered throughout the Illinois District. The Kansas-Missouri area was administered through Forts Kaskaskia, Chartres, Orleans, Cavagnial, and unnamed lesser posts, as a sort of sub-district of the Illinois.

The judicial hierarchy started with the post commandant (who doubled as a sort of sheriff-magistrate). The first commandant of Fort de Cavagnial, for example, was required to "maintain peace among the French and safety in the posts" and to "pursue fugitives." The traders were to "appeal to the commander of the post in case of dissension among the French or among the savage nations on the entire Missouri territory." The commander was also directed to "do justice to them" (the traders) with regard to their contractual rights against *voyageurs* to whom they extended sub-licenses. Formal trial de novo was apparently afforded before the Chief Clerk of the Marine at the Illinois who was civil judge of that district (and apparently at a later date, before the commissaire ordonnateur). The Illinois tribunal appears to have been a court of record. From this court, appeal lay to the Superior Council at New Orleans, composed of a chief judge and several associates. That body was supplied with a clerk *(greffier)* and a crown attorney *(procureur)*. It reviewed transcripts and evidence, read briefs, heard oral arguments, and sometimes heard new evidence. From it, further appeal was occasionally taken to the Privy Council of the Council of State in Paris by a writ in the nature of our certiorari. The Privy Council never examined the facts, and the issues considered were purely questions of law.

Below the appellate level of the Superior Council at New Orleans (where they seem to have been quite active) attorneys appear to have played little part in this system of judicial administration. The only attorney in the Illinois District in the early days was the Royal Notary. Others may have later settled there, and New Orleans attorneys no doubt traveled to the Illinois on occasion. We are told that a standard form book in use was *La Parfait Notaire,* and we have a rather complete picture of the standard law library of private attorneys in New Orleans. The use of attorneys was inveighed against by Governor Vaudreuil in 1751 in no uncertain terms. After charging M. Buchet, Chief Clerk of the Marine at the Illinois, with "judging law suits which may arise among the French," he directed the Sieur de Macarty, the Illinois Commandant, to settle as many as possible "by the method of accommodation" adding somewhat testily:

. . . it being of infinite consequence to prevent the spirit of chicanery being introduced in new settlements. For that reason he [Macarty] will oppose so far as he can the inhabitants employing proctors [attorneys] in their disputes, whose subtleties would become of dangerous consequence.

What was the system of law which governed mid-America (including present Kansas City) under this judicial hierarchy with ever-strengthening effect for nearly a century prior to 1763—and to a lesser degree for more than one-half century thereafter? In essence it was an amalgam of Germanic and Roman law—the substantive customary law of the Franks upon which was grafted a veneer of procedure and organization from the jus civile of ancient Rome. France was a penumbra area in the great conflict of the Germanic and Roman cultures. After Rome fell, the area roughly south of the Loire remained the *pays de droit ecrit*—the land of written (Roman) law—while the center and north of France became the *pays coutumiers*—the land of unwritten or customary (Germanic) law. In the mid-eighteenth century there were some sixty *coutumes generales* applying to large areas such as provinces, and about three hundred *coutumes locales* in particular cities or villages. One of the oldest and most respected of these was the *Coutume de Paris,* the Custom of Paris. This code, during the fourteenth and early fifteenth centuries, gradually came to be a body of written law for Paris and its environs, and it was administered there in the Court of Chaletet under a code of procedure, the Ordinance Civile, established in 1667 by Louis XIV. By an edict of Louis XIV issued September 14, 1712 ("Crozat's Grant"), this custom was made the law of the land in all of Louisiana, which, of course, included the present Kansas-Missouri area. However, it was followed by common consent long before that.

Strangely enough, there appears to be no published English translation extant of the Custom of Paris in spite of the fact that it was (in varying degrees) the law of the land for one-third of the present United States for nearly a century and one-half! A full exposition of it would not be within the scope of this chapter in any event. The Custom of Paris dealt with private (i.e., civil) law and not with criminal law. Some idea of its scope can be ascertained from the abbreviated subject titles listed hereinbelow:

I-II	Feudal Law	VIII	Judgment, execution and attachment
III	Movables and Immovables	IX	Servitudes
IV	Possession	X	Community property
V	Personal actions and mortgages	XI	Dower
VI	Prescription	XII	Guardianship
VII	Re-acquisition of family property sold to an outsider	XIII	Donations
		XIV	Testaments and administration
		XV	Succession
		XVI	Auction sales

These titles include some procedural provisions. Lacking are provisions on contracts (obligations), marriage, paternity, filiation, and criminal law. A good commentary on the development of a large part of the custom is given in the following quotation from an eminent French historian:

> The effects of the Roman law were felt unequally in the various departments of the law. The one which changed the least was the private law as it concerned the family and inheritance. The customs of the north of France maintained the principle of community of possessions between married couples, the widow's dower, the equal division of inheritances between children, and the limitation of the right of testatorship, which have passed into the French Civil Code from the Customs of Paris.

Let us turn to some of the specific incidents involving the application of this law in the days when the country for hundreds of miles in all directions from the present greater

Kansas City area was a part of French-speaking *Haute Loui-siane.*

Probably the most tangible items of a legal nature which survived from the French colonial period in Kansas are the texts of two instruments which fall into the general categories of "contract" and "promissory note" respectively. They appear to represent the oldest legal instruments executed in Kansas of which we have any record. They may have been preceded by a few written *engagé* contracts, but none of these are still extant. They were signed in Fort de Cavagnial on December 9, 1751, by the two principals, Chapuis and Feuilli, of the ill-starred Chapuis expedition. This enterprise started out as a well-manned trading trip to Santa Fe under the quasi-official auspices of the French crown and ended with the desertion of all but the two leaders, the confiscation of their goods at Santa Fe, and their imprisonment for life in Cadiz, Spain. The contract mentioned above recited the general nature of the undertaking, which was a sort of joint venture and was signed by both Chapuis and Feuilli. The note (payable in beaver skins!) was given by Feuilli to Chapuis, apparently for goods advanced. We owe their preservation to the arrest of the two traders and the diligence of the Spanish officials in taking and preserving their depositions and attaching all of their personal papers as evidence. The full text of these two highly interesting instruments is set out hereinbelow, and it should be kept in mind that their present form is an English rendition of a Spanish translation of the French originals.

The contract (which of course was written in longhand) read as follows:

We, Juan Chapuis and Luis Foissy, who have signed below, confess to have formed a company to go together to Spain [sic] with the obligation of reaching, during the month of April, approximately, the location of the Panis Mahas, a place called Santa Bacos. The said Chapuis promises to forward to the said Foissy the sum of four hundred pounds in merchandise to make the journey to Spain under the condition that, if he repudiates what is agreed upon, he will be obliged to pay another fifty pounds, and that the present paper will serve as the obligation. Thus Juan Chapuis signed. The said Foissy has declared that he does not know how to write nor sign his name. He has made his accustomed sign in the presence of the witnesses below. Cavagnol, December 9, 1751. Sign of Foissy X. Juan Chapuis. Pedro Truteau, Lorenzo Truteau, Witnesses.

The text of the note was as follows:

In the presence of witnesses, I, Luis Foissy, who signed below, recognize and confess that I owe Senor Chapuis the amount of four hundred and nine pounds, which sum I promise to pay to the said Chapuis, or at his order, in the month of April next, in beaver skins or others at the price of the merchants of this post. The said Foissy has made his usual sign, not knowing how to write or sign his name. In the Fort of Cavagnol, December 9, 1751. Sign of Foissy X. Pedro Truteau, Lorenzo Truteau, Witnesses.

One wonders who was the scrivener of these instruments. He showed some knowledge of both legal form and business exigencies. Was it Chapuis? Was it the Commandant of the Post, Baron Portneuf? Or perhaps one of the knowledgeable traders who headquartered at the fort? Did he have the benefit of *La Parfait Notaire?* Some day we may be able to throw more light on these transactions by locating the original instruments and comparing the handwriting in the text with the various signatures.

In the field of real estate, we know that Bourgmont was given certain proprietary rights at Fort Orleans in his commission as Commandant of the Missouri. However, this was essentially in the nature of a military order. The first true lease of real estate in our area appears to have been the one granted by Governor Vaudreuil to the *congé* Deruisseau with regard to Fort de Cavagnial on August 8, 1744 (the full text of which is still extant). This was a lease in every sense of the word, specifying a five-year term, referring to Deruisseau et al. as the "tenants," setting out the annual rent they were to pay, describing the premises (in particular Fort de Cavagnial but with appurtenant rights of exploitation of the surrounding area) ensuring them quiet possession of a sort, and requiring that they "shall return, at the expiration of their lease and in good condition, . . . all the buildings (of the fort) mentioned above."

In the treaty of cession after the Louisiana Purchase, France sought to protect the French-speaking people who had received grants under the French and Spanish regimes, by providing for perfection of their claims. Accordingly, statutes were adopted to carry out this program of perfecting land titles. One of the first was enacted March 2, 1805 (2 U.S. Statute 324) for the more settled rural areas, giving heads of families who held a Franco-Spanish patent or order of survey or permit full title to their land. The statute was not particularly adapted to small village lots, and on June 13, 1812 a special statute (2 U.S. Statute 748) was adopted specifically confirming the ownership of the "town or village lots, out lots, common field lots and commons" of the inhabitants of the French villages in the territory of Missouri which had been granted by the French or Spanish authorities. The claims were to be allowed to the extent of "eight hundred arpens, French measure" and many claims stated in arpen[t]s and leagues were thereafter confirmed. Since many of the French settlers moved to their granted lands across the Mississippi after the treaty of cession, including the new lands to the west nearer the present Kansas City area, they could not qualify as having timely settled their Franco-Spanish grants and so a third statute (and later two more like it) was passed on February 5, 1816 (2 U.S. Statute 797) giving them priority or "pre-emption" rights in purchasing their settled land. These statutes all referred to "settlers," and since the French and Spanish authorities had typically granted a 40-arpent tract running back from a river or stream, such tracts came to be referred to generically as "settlers' tracts."

The measure of real estate used by the French was the *arpent* or "Paris acre" which according to Black's *Law Dictionary,* Third Edition, is: "A French measure of land, containing one hundred square perches, of eighteen feet each, or about an acre." Missouri title examiners are quite familiar with the term and usually shorten it to "arpen." Generally, the French in all of Louisiana laid out their fields in long strips, of varying numbers of arpents, extending back from the rivers and streams. There still exist to this day in the bottomland across from the old Amoureaux House in Ste. Genevieve, Missouri, such cultivated strips, bordered by a few ancient pecan trees. The Recorder of Deeds office of Ste. Genevieve County still carries the original entries in the chain of title to much of the surrounding land in terms of so many arpents.

It is interesting to speculate whether some of the land around Forts Orleans and Cavagnial may have been laid out in arpents. A map of Fort Orleans and environs shows some well-defined lots and fields, and these may well have been measured in arpents, the most common measure of land then in use. The French real estate usage (and, indeed, much of the French law) was continued under the Spanish administration in Louisiana, and there is evidence that grants of land as late as the early 1800s were expressed in terms of arpents. It is, therefore, highly possible that the grants of land in 1795 to the previously mentioned colony of French farmers below Wolf River (at Montain Creek near present Highland in Doniphan County in the old Spanish District of St. Charles), if they could be located, would be phrased in terms of arpents. The colony lasted only two years and left no records, so far as we know. But while it survived, the dim echo of the Custom of Paris no doubt had some influence on the relationships of the French-speaking inhabitants of this little corner of Kansas.

Also, the pre-Chouteau French-speaking squatters along the Kaw River in the old French Bottoms of Kansas City (about where the stockyards are now located) no doubt thought of their farms in terms of arpents, although they probably abjured legal formalities. The location and spacing of the tracts on Father Point's 1840 French map of Kansas City would certainly seem to allow for arpent strips along the Missouri and on either side of Turkey Creek. Two 40 arpent "settlers' tracts" in the West Bottoms are fairly apparent from the old land records. The Missouri real estate statutes expressly refer to and adopt the *Livre Terrein*, Volume I of which contained the numerous arpent grants made during the French regime. The first thirty or so volumes of the Missouri Supreme Court reports contain innumerable cases litigating title to these arpent tracts. One of these involved 30,000 arpents granted to Pierre Chouteau in 1799 west of present Boonville on the Missouri River, and there may have been others even closer to (or within) the Kansas City area. An early-day writer on Kansas City French history, Garraghan, mentions arpent tracts.

It is rather intriguing to consider that every landholder in Kansas City and the surrounding Missouri-Kansas area holds title by mesne conveyances of one sort or another from Louis XIV. The chain of title reads something like this: Louis XIV's title to Louisiana was perfected by formal declaration and actual possession taken by La Salle in 1682; Louis XV took by right of monarchical succession from Louis XIV in 1715 (subject temporarily to the Regency); Louis XV ceded Louisiana to Spain in 1762; Spain retroceded to France in 1800; France, per Napoleon, ceded to the U.S. in 1803; and present titles by and large date from the U.S. patents or railroad grants based upon this acquisition.

It will be recalled that feudal law comprised the first two titles of the Custom of Paris, listed above, which once applied to this area. While feudal tenures do not appear to have been granted in our region, it is worthy of note that at least two

residents of Kansas during the mid-1700s held feudal seig-
niories in Canada. They no doubt continued to look after these
interests and exercise their feudal prerogatives while living on
the Missouri. One of these gentlemen was the first trader at
Fort de Cavagnial, M. Deruisseau, whom Governor Vaudreuil
described in his *congé* papers as "seigneur en partie de l'isle
Perrot en Canada." The other was Robineau de Portneuf,
third commandant of the same post, who was lord of a
seigniory along the St. Lawrence known as Neuf de la Poterie,
and whom the chronicler Bossu (who knew him personally)
always referred to as "Baron Portneuf." While on the subject
of royal grants, it bears mentioning that Bourgmont, the
French explorer who founded Fort Orleans and negotiated the
Comanche treaty, was awarded a title of nobility by Louis
XV—the only such title awarded for services in the Missouri-
Kansas area. His coat of arms, prepared by the King's master
of heraldry, portrayed a plains Indian against a background of
silver mountains (the Rockies) under an azure sky.

One cannot ignore the fact that the institution of slavery was
not only legal but also actively carried on in Missouri, and in
all probability in Kansas as well, during the French period.
There is frequent mention of slaves in the reports of the
Superior Council dealing with Upper Louisiana. A whole
body of law, the *Code Noir* ("Black Code") was adopted by the
French to deal with the subject. This was the "Edict Concerning the Negro Slaves in Louisiana" issued by Louis XV in
March, 1724. The thrust of the code was actually humanitari-
an. (Article III of this same code decreed a state church
[Roman Catholic] for all Louisiana, including the Missouri-
Kansas area.) One of the letters found by the Spanish among
the Chapuis expedition papers was from one Languenin and
dated December 7, 1751, at "Fort Cavagnol" in present
Kansas, asking the recipient (apparently Feuilli) to join in
"recovering the slave which I have sold to him." The preface to
the *1855 Territorial Statutes of Kansas* devotes considerable space
in an attempt to explain away such history (which constituted

at that time a very embarrassing precedent to the "free-staters"), by trying to show that the French law was never really in effect in Kansas.

The French also tried prohibition of a sort (with about the same success as greeted a similar measure nearly two centuries later). In the wide-open "frontier days" of the early 1700s, Bourgmont's men had made wine with impunity from wild grapes at the Kansa village north of present Fort Leavenworth. But in the instrument authorizing Fort de Cavagnial, Governor Vaudreuil forbade the sale by the traders of "any drinks such as wine, brandy, or other intoxicating liquors" under pain of "corporal punishment" for violators. While the regulation was designed primarily to prevent sales of such potables to the Indians, it was also enforced by the Illinois Commandant with regard to sales to the garrisons in the frontier forts. It was a breach of this regulation forbidding traders to carry liquor which led to the first recorded homicide on Kansas soil to be later followed by a formal judicial proceeding and execution. As we have seen in a previous chapter, two Canadian *voyageurs*, on February 24, 1751, stopped at Fort de Cavagnial. Among their goods was a plentiful supply of brandy, some of which they sold to a soldier of the garrison, whose name we do not know. The soldier became thoroughly drunk and proceeded to murder his commanding officer, Lieutenant Augustin-Antoine de la Barre, Seigneur de Jardin. This young gentleman, a protegé of the governor, was the husband of Marie-Anne Adhemar de Lantagnac, a cousin of Governor Vaudreuil of Louisiana and grandniece of Vaudreuil's father who was then Governor of Canada. The accused, being in the military, was immediately arrested and sent to the Illinois headquarters, where on March 18, 1751 he was tried before a Council of War and shot. The two *voyageurs* who had sold the intoxicants to him were summarily imprisoned. The full record of the crime and the later trial at Illinois was sent to Paris by Governor Vaudreuil but appears not to have survived in the archives. It should be mentioned that this proceeding was strictly military, in the nature of a court martial, and not within the ambit of the Custom of Paris, which was purely a civil code.

The "long arm of the law" was seemingly a part of the administration of justice even among the military posts of colonial France in mid-America. In 1753, Baron Portneuf, commandant of Fort de Cavagnial, reported that four soldiers had deserted from Fort de Cavagnial. It so happened, however, that the Wichita Indians, toward whom the deserters fled, were firm allies of the French, and their grand village flew the ancient white Bourbon flag of the lilies of France. One senses from the military dispatch that an aboriginal *posse comitatus* materialized among the Wichita upon receipt of the report concerning the four deserters. In any event, Macarty, Commandant at the Illinois, reported in his dispatch to Governor Vaudreuil that the four had been killed by the Wichita, adding laconically that it would therefore not seem to be necessary to fill out the "usual reports" concerning their desertion.

Larceny was a not uncommon crime in the French period, and it was frequently practiced by the Indians (since the goods of the *voyageurs* proved quite irresistible to some of them). However, they generally accompanied their booty with the *voyageur's* scalp so there were few witnesses, and fewer trials. On one occasion the Missouri were so bold as to undertake a horse-stealing expedition right to the gates of Fort de Cavagnial. Two of them were killed outright by the garrison, but the rest escaped, leaving little for a chronicler of history to report, other than the fact of this audacious foray. Incidentally, these seem to have been the only shots "fired in anger" from Kansas' first fort.

It may come as a surprise to many to learn that the law of community property (which is still in effect in several southern and western states with a French or Spanish heritage) once obtained in the Kansas-Missouri area comprising metropolitan Kansas City. Since a translation of this particular part of the Custom of Paris is readily available, pertinent excerpts from it are hereinafter set out (using Article numbers current in 1746):

ARTICLE CCXX.—Concerning the property that enters into the community and the time when the community begins.

Men and women united by marriage own in common all movable property, and the immovable property acquired during their uninterrupted marriage. And the community begins from the day of the marriage and nuptial benediction. [This article is No. 100 of the Ancient Customs.]

ARTICLE CCXXIX.—Division of the community.

After the death of one of the said spouses the community property is divided as follows: the surviving spouse takes one-half, and the heirs of the deceased spouse take the other half.

Other articles dealt with continuation of the community in default of a valid inventory upon death of a spouse, closing the inventory after three months, and continuation of the community (by thirds) upon remarriage of the surviving spouse—the children taking one-third, and the husband and wife one-third each.

An interesting case involving this part of the custom arose in the Kansas-Missouri area and was tried at the Illinois and appealed to the Superior Council in New Orleans. The case was *Thibierge* v. *Marin,* and it is amply documented because of the appeal, which was heard on March 5, 1746. One Sergeant Dubois, after accompanying Bourgmont on his trip to negotiate the great Comanche treaty in western Kansas in 1724, had married Francoise Missoury, the celebrated Princess of the Missouris at Notre Dame Cathedral in Paris, upon Bourgmont's gala return to France. Dubois was killed by Indians after the couple returned to the Missouri country (where they lived for a time at Fort Orleans) but was survived by children, one of whom married Thibierge, the plaintiff. Dubois' widow married Louis Marin de la Marque, the defendant, and had

children by him. The trial in the lower court was held at the
Illinois on April 2, 1745, the issue there being whether the
children of the first marriage (to Dubois) were entitled to a
share in the "community" created by the marriage of the
widow to her second husband (Marin). She had died prior to
commencement of the suit. The theory of the action was that
the widow Dubois had failed to properly inventory the
community property existing with regard to Dubois upon his
death and by commingling the same with the property in the
new community with Marin, had thereby continued the old
marital community, in which the children born of the Dubois
marriage (and their issue) were entitled to share.

The Council found that a purported inventory made at the
time of Dubois' death was not in the form required by the
Custom of Paris, distinguished a decree of 1601 urged by
Marin which upheld an inventory on somewhat similar facts,
and found a continuation of the old Dubois marital community. In accordance with the Custom of Paris, the property was
divided one-third to the children of Dubois, one-third to
Marin, and one-third to be divided in equal shares between
the children of Dubois and the children of Marin. The opinion
makes an interesting reference to an attached exhibit consisting of "a contract of July 10, 1734 between Pichard and Marin
relative to transfer of cattle from Missouri to Illinois, signed by
Marin and by R. P. Tartarin." This early contract appears not
to have survived in the records.

Another case in the Superior Council reports for the March
5, 1746 session had to do with the law of persons and involved a
gentleman closely associated, for a time, with the geographical
area in which we are interested. The case was *Portneuf* v.
Trudeau. Louis Robineau de Portneuf commanded at Fort
Orleans for a time, later was stationed at the Illinois, and
eventually became the most well known commandant at Fort
de Cavagnial. While at the Illinois, he married the widow of la
Buissonniere, a former Commandant there. By virtue of this
marriage (or in connection therewith) he became tutor

(guardian) of the minor son of his wife by her first husband. The litigation which reached the Superior Council had to do with an issue which arose over the property of the minor. Portneuf had been removed as tutor in favor of Trudeau, the boy's maternal uncle, and objected to the latter's insistence that he be paid the proceeds of the minor's patrimony at the old pre-inflation currency rates. (Portneuf lost.)

Both the Thibierge and Portneuf cases illustrate the fact that a married woman was a *femme couvert* under the civil law and any action touching her interests had to be brought (or at least joined in) by her baron, i.e., husband. Our familiar "married women's acts" had no place in French law in the 1700s. It is also of interest to note that marriages were entered into by virtue of a written contract drawn up by the notary and signed by the principals and witnesses.

Although no legal proceedings were involved, Portneuf illustrates in another situation the fact that the institution of advancing of credit and delinquency in the repayments of same are universal in human societies. Portneuf had borrowed (or perhaps received trade goods advanced) from one Monsieur Olivier at the Illinois prior to 1751. Portneuf, as we have noted, went to Fort de Cavagnial in 1751 (replacing the murdered La Barre). He became delinquent in repayment and about every dispatch from Governor Vaudreuil in New Orleans to Illinois Commandant Macarty urged him to see that Portneuf paid his debt to M. Olivier. One notes in passing that the governor wrote a very good collection letter. It is also rather amusing to reflect on the difficulties of communicating with debtors in those days. Macarty wrote from the Illinois, in a response to one of Vaudreuil's pleas, advising that the Missouri River was frozen that winter, and that there would be a delay of several months in forwarding the governor's dunning letter to Portneuf. Macarty promised that he would send the letter with the first traders ascending the river in the spring. Macarty wrote in late 1752, with obvious relief, that the obligation had been satisfied in full.

While we know of no wills actually written in our immediate area during the French period, the Kansas-western Missouri area was indirectly involved and perhaps in a way responsible for, one will following the French form (written during the nominal Spanish control of the Illinois). St. Ange de Bellerieve came to Missouri and Kansas as Bourgmont's second in command during the Comanche expedition of 1723 and stayed on for several years as Commandant of Fort Orleans. One François Villiers came to Kansas in 1744 as first commandant of Fort de Cavagnial and stayed until about 1749. Villiers returned to the Illinois, where he met and married the sister of St. Ange. St. Ange himself never married, was later stationed at Vincennes and Fort Chartres, and then lived in St. Louis after 1765. On December 26, 1774, St. Ange died at St. Louis, leaving a typical French will (the full text of which has been preserved) which gave all of his estate to the Villiers children. Such French wills were drawn by the notary and customarily recited (as St. Ange's did) that "death is certain, and the time of its coming very uncertain," contained lengthy intercessions to divinity and all "the saints of the celestial Court" to place the testator's soul in the "Kingdom of the Blessed," provided for burial and masses, and concluded with the details of disposition of the testator's estate. The lure of mid-America to France brought these individuals here in the first place, and no doubt some of St. Ange's estate was accumulated as the result of his participation in the great expedition via present Kansas City to the Comanches in western Kansas (Bourgmont having received his previously mentioned title of nobility for leading it) and his long stay at Fort Orleans.

Even as long ago as the 1700s the French colonial government in the Kansas-Missouri area took a hand in the economics of commerce and engaged in a degree of government control of business. As a result there were certain "white collar crimes" even in those days! For example, Governor Vaudreuil, in his directive authorizing Fort de Cavagnial, noted that the

voyageurs were "competing with one another by giving away
their goods at very low prices, and even selling them at a loss,
which would bring about the voyageurs' ruin, and also prevent
commerce from increasing." To those who are familiar with
present-day price control and fair trade legislation, these
words will have a familiar ring. The Kansa Indians told the
French authorities in 1752 that there must be some governmental control "to avoid the uproar of the voyageurs who
snatch a beaver pelt from each other." Vaudreuil's answer to
these economic problems in 1744 was to issue a *congé* (an old
French legal term signifying a license) to a superintendent-
trader, Deruisseau, who would have a monopoly and issue
sub-franchises for trade on the entire Missouri River. He was
to see that prices were kept at a suitable level, that no
unlicensed traders poached on his province, and that the
traders did not take advantage of their red-skinned customers.
The *congé's* privileges were to be supported by the commandant and garrison at Fort de Cavagnial, whose expenses he was
to pay in the form of a "gratuity."

There is a recorded case of a rather spectacular free
enterpriser, one Avion, who in 1752 ignored the government-
sponsored monopoly and, incredibly, persuaded the *entire*
Kansa grand village to leave the location of Fort de Cavagnial
and to settle near his trading station "lower down, on the
Kansa," i.e., somewhere near the metropolitan area of Kansas
City. He thus gained the distinction of being the first known
businessman in the Kansas City area. This caused great
consternation at Fort de Cavagnial, since the traders there
could no longer sell their goods to the Kansa, and the
commandant was unable to collect his "gratuity" from any of
them. Avion's forestalling adventure was short-lived, however,
and in less than a year the Kansa returned to the fort. Of M.
Avion, we have no further record.

Another item worthy of note is somewhat indirectly related
to French law and its enforcement in the Kansa and western
Missouri area. The first *congé* at Fort de Cavagnial—the man

charged by Governor Vaudreuil with carrying out his plans for commerce and working with the commandant there in "keeping the peace" and enforcing the traders' contracts—was the same Lefebvre-Deruisseau who was later the first civil judge of St. Louis, and in a sense of all Missouri (and Kansas). In other words, Missouri's first judge may have gained a good deal of his practical experience in Kansas and in close proximity to the present Kansas City area. Governor St. Ange, when he removed the seat of French authority from Fort de Chartres in present Illinois to St. Louis in 1765, appointed Judge Lefebvre (already serving as such at Fort de Chartres) as civil judge of the new community and of the handful of other little French communities in the Illinois area on the west side of the Mississippi. With St. Ange, Judge Lefebvre signed the first fifteen real estate titles in St. Louis, which were duly recorded in the *Livre Terrein.* His signature, with St. Ange's, also appears as commissaire ordonnateur on the *procès verbal,* by which Fort de Chartres below St. Louis, and all its appurtenances, was turned over to the British. This was without question the most important single real estate instrument executed in the Midwest up to that time. A copy is on display in the museum at Fort de Chartres.

One of Judge Lefebvre's cases is reported in Billon's *Annals of St. Louis.* A French trader had been captured by the Indians and a shipment of goods destined for him was landed at Ste. Genevieve. Judge Lefebvre, the notary, and the attorney for vacant estates (a sort of public administrator) of the "Royal Jurisdiction of Illinois" went to Ste. Genevieve, duly received and inventoried the goods, and "after maturely considering the circumstances" placed them in protective custody with a local man of good repute.

While there is a wealth of material on French law in the eighteenth century and on its application at the Illinois, and even more so in Lower Louisiana, I have tried to confine this chapter to those few little-known instances where it in some way touched the Kansas-western Missouri area. I have already outlined the chronology of the beginnings of that law in our area, and it might be of interest to do likewise regarding its twilight period. After promulgation of the Treaty of Paris in 1763, the Spanish control of the French communities on the western side of the Mississippi in upper Louisiana was late in coming, never very enthusiastic, and mostly nominal. By and large, French civil law continued to govern much of the lives of the inhabitants, with a few Spanish overtones here and there when the Spanish statutes were enforced. The garrison at Fort de Cavagnial did not leave the fort until the spring of 1764, and there was no Spanish garrison in St. Louis until 1769. In all probability squatters continued to occupy what was left of the fort for some time. Because of the high percentage of French in the population, French law was practiced and French-speaking judges were of necessity appointed in Missouri until well into the nineteenth century. There were only a few non-Frenchmen in St. Louis in 1805, and the population there was overwhelmingly French as late as 1825 when General Lafayette paid a visit. The same, of course, was even more true of the then remote area which was later destined to be Greater Kansas City.

When the "Territory of New Orleans" was organized in 1804, the upper part of Louisiana became the "District of Louisiana" and was made subject to the governor of Indiana. In 1805 the area was renamed "Territory of Louisiana" and given its own government. In 1812, it was reorganized again and named "Territory of Missouri." The laws then in effect in the area were continued by this series of statutes. Since these laws were, up to that time, French (and Spanish) laws, the civil law was therefore continued in both Missouri and Kansas for a considerable time. The preface to the *Statutes of Kansas Territory* takes pains to discuss the history of civil law in Louisiana at some length but surmises (somewhat incorrectly) that there probably had not been any Frenchmen in Kansas to whom it could apply. This was probably more a function of free-state embarrassment regarding the *Code Noir* than a reflection of

historical accuracy. As we have seen, there were indeed many
Frenchmen, some women, their slaves, chattels, commerce,
and real estate to which these laws applied. It was not until
January 19, 1816 that what little vitality the French civil law
had was formally ended in the Missouri area by a statute of
Missouri Territory adopting the common law of England.
After Missouri became a state in 1821, Kansas lapsed into
somewhat of a penumbra area, and it was not until February
11, 1859, that the Legislative Assembly of the then Territory of
Kansas also adopted the common law of England as the law of
the land. With this act died any shadow of authority or
customary usage of the French civil law. As late as 1909,
however, the Missouri Supreme Court refused to follow the
presumption that the common law was in effect in Kansas,
saying that "this presumption is indulged as to those states
only that have taken the common law as a basis of their
jurisprudence." The court noted that Kansas had formerly
been subject to the laws of France and that "the common law
never existed in Kansas, without it has been adopted by
statute" (which 1859 statute counsel had unfortunately failed
to plead).

Interestingly enough, when the English common law swept
into our area with the rising tide of Yankee territorial
immigration, it brought with it a residuum of "law French"
whose origin was essentially the same as that of the law of
colonial France in Upper Louisiana. Britain was conquered in
1066 by the Norman French ancestors of the Norman French
who originally colonized much of central North America.
"Law French" had thus become entrenched as the language of
the courts in England and did not fully wane until the
seventeenth century. The "Records in English" Statute,
directed against law French, was passed as late as 1731. By that
time, however, "the law French tide had ebbed, leaving words
and phrases stranded in English." Thus French terms such as
marriage, purchase, infant, property, devise, pardon, constable, larceny,
attorney, judge, evidence, replevin, verdict, and *warrant* are heard in

Kansas City in the American courts of *Haute Louisiane* once again, imported from France by way of England.

Both Kansas and Missouri have long and illustrious histories of judicial administration under the English common law. But these histories are really "older than their years" for they extend back under the French civil law for a century or more before the time when Missouri became a state, and a century and one-half before Kansas did so. Not only does this civil law background lend a certain patina to our legal history, but it contributed in a very material way to our civilization. For the settlers of the Midwest did not really found a civilization—they built upon the foundations of an older French culture, whose existence made empire-building a much easier job. Although we did not inherit the laws of that culture, it left us a legacy perhaps equally as important as the mere form of the substantive law. The inhabitants along the Missouri River—trappers, traders, farmers, and Indians—were accustomed to the civilizing influence of the rule of law, and that law in their era was the civil law of France and ancient Rome. We are the beneficiaries of that salutary influence.

CHAPTER V

The French Spaniards
And the Fur Trade

IN SPITE OF THE NOMINAL TAKE-OVER of Louisiana by the
Spanish in 1763, the Illinois country, and particularly the area
upriver along the Missouri to present Kansas City and beyond,
remained overwhelmingly French. The entire early population of St. Louis was made up of Frenchmen who moved over
from the French settlements on the eastern side of the
Mississippi. Until 1770, St. Ange, the former officer of Bourgmont, acted as Commandant at St. Louis, and even after he
was relieved by Piernas, the Spanish commandant, there were
never more than a handful of Spanish military and government personnel there. The few Spanish nationals who did
venture to St. Louis were faced with the discouraging restric-
tions of Spain's mercantilistic policies. Meriwether Lewis
reported in 1803 of "the Spanish being so few in number that
they deserve no notice as a special class of people."

From St. Louis came the *fermiers* or major traders for furs
whose business extended far up the Missouri. Their names
were for the most part typically French: Laclede, Chouteau,
Cerre, Perrault, Martigny, and Clamorgan were prominent
ones. The official list of all traders granted licenses in the
Illinois in 1792 showed seventeen principal traders, of whom
fifteen were listed as of French nationality, one as Spanish, and
one as "Mestizo." And even though a Spanish name or two
crept into the roster of traders' permits in the later period, the

engagés—who actually took the goods upriver, conducted the trading, and brought the furs down—were almost exclusively French. Since *engagés'* names did not appear on the licenses to be discussed later in this chapter, it may be interesting to note some of them here, for example: Francois Marc, Thomas Benir, Sans Chagrin, Claude Roussel dit "Sans Souci," Pierre Oliver dit "Bellepeche," De Coigne, Tous Gaillard, Muslin Barb, Du Chemin, Anti Regis, La Margullier, Azeau dit "Berthoud," Sans Quartier, Langlois dit "Rondeau," Blanchette la Chasseur and a host of others. The "dit" in a name above signifies a sobriquet. This was largely due to the fact that they were half-breeds or thoroughgoing coureurs de bois who, after the usual Indian fashion, had adopted a nickname. Usually the *engagé* established an entrepôt of some sort near the tribe with which he traded and sent out hunters and trappers, both Indian and French, to harvest the furs and bring them in for the winter's trading.

As will be seen in both this chapter and the next, there is ample evidence that many such entrepôts, from a mere hole or "cache" in the ground, on up to thatch huts and perhaps even more permanent structures made of logs, were from time to time established in the vicinity of Kansas City by the French traders during the "Spanish" period. While there are a few gaps in the record, we can come quite close to tracing the list of the traders to the Kansa nation all the way from Deruisseau's first *congé* privileges at Fort de Cavagnial in 1744 down to François Chouteau's Kansa trading station at present Kansas City in 1821! After the abandonment of Fort de Cavagnial and the founding of St. Louis, the record is quite well documented. Laclede himself seems to have retained the entire Missouri River trade, including that of the Kansa, in the early years. Through varying periods of exclusive licenses, open trade, and sharing in trade by lots, the chronological list is approximately as follows:

Marin   1728-1736

Joseph Deruisseau	1745-1750
Despins and Larche	1752
Pierre Laclede Liguest	1765-1777
(Trade sporadic due to British-sponsored Indian depredations)	1775-1783
A. Chouteau, Labbadie, Cerre	1778
A. Chouteau	1786
A. Chouteau (and Commandant Perez, St. Louis)	1790
Pierre Chouteau (as *engagé* for A. Chouteau or Picote de Beletre)	1791
Open trade on the Missouri	1792
No trade due to Osage War	1793
Commandant Zenon Trudeau and Benito Vasquez, Bernal Sarpy, and Laurent Durocher	1794
Bonaventura Collell, Benito Vasquez, Quenache de Rouin (and 3 others)	1795
Six licensees, drawn by lot	1796
Six licensees, drawn by lot	1797
Sarpy Brothers	1798
Gregoire Sarpy and Cabanne	1799
Bernal, Sarpy, Cabanne	1800
Gregoire Sarpy, Cabanne	1801
Clamorgan	1802
Clamorgan	1803
Francis Dorion and Pierre Montardy	1807
Ft. Osage (Government trade monopoly)	1808-1822
No trade due to War with British	1812
François G. Chouteau	1816-1822

The official Spanish reports, interestingly enough, end with the following comment of Commandant Delassus of St. Louis for 1804: "Year 1804—The Devil may take all." The endless intrigues, bickering, and backbiting over the issuance of trade licenses were over for him, for Spain had ceded Louisiana to France and Napoleon had sold it to the fledgling United States. Even so, the immediate Kansas City area remained predominantly a French enclave for nearly another forty years—but that is again getting ahead of our story.

As late as 1785, the Kansa were reported by a Spaniard as still living on the Missouri River "on a very high cliff about two 'avenzadas' from the shore of that river." This was apparently still in the vicinity of their first old village, where they had been located when Fort de Cavagnial was abandoned. However, in 1796 Commandant Trudeau at St. Louis reported that they were "on the river Cans [Kansas] where it divides, 60 leagues from its mouth." There they stayed through the early 1800s and the genesis of Kansas City, until their removal to the Kaw Agency at Council Grove in 1848 and from there eventually to Oklahoma in 1873.

It is apparent from the table above that the Chouteaus, who were to make the first really permanent settlement at Kansas City, had actually been living in or near our area on and off since 1778. At that time Auguste Chouteau was the trader at the Kansa nation located, as just noted, at the site of their first old village (by Fort de Cavagnial). The Chouteaus continued to enjoy the Kansa trading privileges through the 1780s and 1790s. Auguste Chouteau lived during the entire winter of 1790-91 at the Kansa village which had then been moved up the Kaw River a number of miles. There he encountered a well-documented case of international trade rivalry. A party of Sac and Fox Indians arrived from the north with a large supply of English goods, which they proceeded to trade for nearly all of the furs which the Kansa had available. Since Chouteau had hoped to trade his own supply of goods for these furs, he had thus been deprived of an entire season's business. Chouteau's predicament on his trip downriver was further complicated by the fact that the Sac and Foxes, on their way down the Missouri, told the Osage of their exploit and of Chouteau's presence at the Kansa village. This greatly angered the Osage, who had been officially cut off from French trade goods by Governor Miro, due to depredations they had committed. It was only through the strong intervention of the chief of their party that their young men were induced to return to Chouteau's lodge his goods which they had taken. Such were the hazards in those days of the commerce flowing past the future port of Kansas City.

Trading along the Missouri, both above and below present Kansas City, had reached substantial proportions by the 1790s. One M. Mitchell told Alexander Hamilton in 1792 that from 50 to 100 boats navigated the Missouri annually, going as far as 1,200 miles upstream. The first of the more ambitious general fur-trading enterprises, The Missouri Company, was formed at St. Louis on October 15, 1793. Its traders thereafter plied the Missouri past present Kansas City and up as far as the Mandans.

Jean Baptiste Trudeau headed the first expedition of the Missouri Fur Company starting on June 7, 1794. The expedition itself, as reported by Trudeau, makes quite a story, but our interest here is more limited. Trudeau passed the mouth of the Kansas River on July 12. One Jacques d'Eglise, who couldn't have left St. Louis much later than Trudeau (i.e., sometime in June) overtook Trudeau on August 6 and gave him several letters from the director of the company. In one of these, he reported that he was "enjoined to give to Mr. Quenneville, at the entrance of the Kansas River, the 26 trading guns which were entrusted to me." He added, however, that "I was not able to do it, being nearly 100 leagues away from him" (upon receiving the letter August 6). Thus, from June, 1794, when the letter was written, to August, 1794, when Trudeau noted that he was still there, M. Quenneville seems to have been more or less permanently established for company trading business "at the entrance of the Kansas River" i.e., at the present location of Kansas City. Presumably he maintained this entrepôt at the

Kawsmouth rendezvous all summer and must at least have
had a tent or lean-to to protect his goods, since Trudeau
erected such protection even while en route. Another trader,
Quenache de Rouin, was captured by a party of Iowas and
robbed of his goods, clothes, food, and guns in early 1795 and
left at the entrance of the Kansas River where he was later
rescued.

Perrin DuLac, the well-known young Frenchman of letters,
visited the future site of Kansas City in May or June of 1802.
He made at least a primitive start at warehousing here, for
after trading for furs at the Kansas village (then up the Kaw)
he says he "departed for the mouth of the River Kansas, where
we dug a hole, in which we deposited our skins, so that they
might not incommode us in our voyage." Kansas City's future
site was at that time again under French sovereignty.

Two items in the official correspondence of that day give us
an insight into the fact that the Kansa Indians were thoroughly French insofar as their acquired European characteristics
were concerned. In a request for the customary medals and
gorgets to award to the chiefs and captains of the Kansa tribe,
the St. Louis Commandant noted down their picturesque
names, in French, which were as follows: LePetit Chef, Les
grands Chevaux, Le Batard, LeGeur qui brule (Cour qui
Brule), Le petit Maigre, Le Couteau, Le Gauche, Le gendre du
Coupique, Le foulier Monille, and Le gendre de la Butte. And
in the winter of 1800, Cour qui Brule, Chief of the Kansas,
wrote to the Illinois Commandant (in French) recalling that
"for a long time I was the hand and sole support of the
French." He stated that he would descend to St. Louis "at the
melting of the ice," adding "I shall not ask you for any
presents, for I have the heart of a Frenchman, and I am not like
those chiefs who come to see you to obtain presents."

Toward the end of the 1700s and during the first three or
four years of the 1800s, a brief renewal of attempts at the Santa
Fe trade sprang up. Of course, both ends of the trail were then
in Spanish or French-Spanish hands, which made the feat

easier to carry off. Pedro Vial, sent by the Santa Fe commandant for the express purpose of reopening the route, left Taos
and arrived at the Illinois in 1795 by way of the Kansa village,
the Kaw River, and present Kansas City. The extent to which
the Midwest remained essentially French is illustrated by the
fact that none of the Spanish knew the route and the
commandant had been forced to turn to Vial, a Frenchman, to
undertake the trip. French traders at the Kansa village (then
upstream on the Kaw) prevented Vial's loss of everything he
had with him at the hands of obstreperous Kansa braves, and
he made his way down the Kaw, past the future site of Kansas
City and on to St. Louis. Several traders made the same trip
from the Illinois, up the Missouri and thence overland to Santa
Fe in the last years of Spanish control. But the fur trade far
overshadowed these sporadic and feeble mercantile contacts
with Santa Fe. Let us pause in our historical narrative to take a
brief look at this fascinating business, the main preoccupation
of the French-speaking "Spaniards" of mid-America.

Furs were the raison d'être of the Missouri River trade. The
search for them opened up the West and were the first
commerce and money of Kansas City. In the present day we
are so out of touch with this important phase of our early-day
history that we telescope the entire era into a few lackluster
comments about "fur traders"—not really knowing who they
were or what they did. But the fur trade covered a period far
longer than the celebrated Santa Fe trade and rivaled or
exceeded it in annual monetary value during the peak years. It
is said that the fur trade at St. Louis from the Missouri River
watershed annually amounted to $200,000 from 1790 to 1804,
and between $200,000 and $300,000 annually from 1807 to
1847. This was big business. It literally founded and was the
sole support of St. Louis for 75 years and similarly was
responsible for the early exploitation of the Kansas City area
and the eventual founding of the first settlement here.

Since our area and its early French history are so intimately
associated with the fur trade, this seems an appropriate point

for a brief digression on the nature of that trade. Especially so since we have nearly arrived at the point in our chronology when fur trading ceased to be the exclusive enterprise in our area and was gradually superseded by permanent settlements of French-speaking farmers.

The subject of the fur trade is so vast and many-faceted that one could not hope to cover it even in survey form in only one chapter. An admirable two-volume work by Chittenden, *A History of the American Fur Trade of the Far West* served for years as the standard source in this field. It has now been supplanted by the definitive two-volume study *The Fur Trade* by Paul Phillips published by the University of Oklahoma Press (1961). The reader is referred to them for well-written and well-documented background information on the subject.

The *castor* (beaver) trade followed the rhythm of the seasons. Beavers, small rodents, hibernated during the winter, which in much of their North American range could be harsh. Ideally, they needed to start their long winter nap with thick fur for warmth, thicker well-lubricated skin for a weather barrier and a large accumulation of subcutaneous fat for stored energy and further warmth. As the days shortened before the cold season, an automatic metamorphosis occurred and the lean summer animals began to accumulate fat and fur and their skin became glossy. The pelts, consisting of the true or ground hair and long guard hairs (to shed water), were at their best when the heavy frosts began. That was the high season for the fur trappers. As the cycle continued and the beaver came out of hibernation in the spring, they shed their fur, and their skin became thin and tough. The creamy supple skin of the high season turned to a dry, darker color. These were the "blue pelts" of summer, and as James Michener aptly wrote in *Centennial,* the same formerly rich pelt taken in summer was "not worth a sou."

What is the story of the fur trade at Kansas City? It was this area's first agribusiness—the first commercial exploitation of a natural product. We have already touched occasionally upon its extent in time—from the late 1680s until the middle 1800s. The port of Kansas City has been in operation longer than many realize. While no permanent settlement was made here until the late 1700s or early 1800s, Kawsmouth served as a convenient rendezvous point for the fur traders from the earliest days. The first commercial vessels to come up the Missouri to our area were no doubt the hollowed-out cottonwood logs which the French traders used as canoes or pirogues. Later as construction facilities grew up at St. Louis, heavier planked bateaux were used to carry trade goods upriver and furs down. Sometimes two large canoes or pirogues were lashed together somewhat like a catamaran, joined by a flat deck of planks. It was said that such a vessel could carry up to fifteen tons.

Our interest generally centers upon the more colorful phases of the trade involving the Indians and their furs, but it should not escape our attention that although the medium of exchange was furs, and the sellers were aborigines, a tremendous commerce in manufactured European trade articles was built up from about 1700 on, which was a fully developed mercantile system involving sizeable outlays of capital and necessitating development of provisioning, warehousing, financing, insuring, etc. St. Louis was the headquarters of this business: Kansas City and the regions upriver were the field of activity. As the Indians (and French) became more sophisticated in their tastes and needs, this trade took on more and more of a modern mercantile character and the Chouteaus' trading houses in St. Louis and Kansas City formed a direct link with the mercantile houses of today. The stream of goods flowing past the future site of Kansas City grew ever larger over the years. We know that 100 packs of skins (mostly beaver) were sent downriver from Fort de Cavagnial in 1757, a prolific quantity for that day. The trade grew to such proportions that in 1809 Manuel Lisa's trading expedition to the upper Missouri consisted of 350 men (at least one-half French Creole in the trading section). The group was transported in a flotilla of thirteen keelboats and barges.

The furs which were the subject of this trade were for the most part the high-grade Rocky Mountain beaver, although others were collected. Governor Vandreuil's 1744 charter for Fort de Cavagnial provided:

> They will be permitted to take to Canada the furs enumerated hereafter, i.e., beavers, martens, peckans and other furs which will not be a threat to its commerce, and to bring back to this country (Louisiana) the product of the sale, in goods fit for trade on this Missouri River. Said fermiers will be required to bring down to New Orleans all the other hides such as deer, roe-buck, cow (buffalo) all of these, in short, which would be more profitable to commerce in this province.

Chittenden listed standard packs of furs in the later years as follows:

> A pack of furs contained ten buffalo robes, fourteen bear, sixty otter, eighty beaver, eighty raccoon, one hundred and twenty foxes, or six hundred muskrat skins.

As Chittenden notes, there were two very dissimilar methods of obtaining furs, and by and large they represented two separate periods of trade. The first, and the one generally employed during the French period, consisted of exchanging trade goods acquired by the trader for the furs which had been collected by the Indians. The French generally recognized tacitly the proprietary rights of the Indians and did not trap on their lands. After the cession of Louisiana to the United States, this attitude gradually changed and the second method arose, consisting of large-scale direct trapping on Indian lands without the payment of trade goods either for the furs or for the right to trap them.

Since the system of collection by the Indians was the one principally in use during the French period, its characteristics are of interest to us. As anyone knows who has skinned a rabbit or squirrel or raccoon, the fur trade was a messy business at times. After catching a beaver (which was an art in itself), the Indians would slit the belly of the animal and the inside of its four legs, carefully remove the skin, and dry it on a willow hoop. Later the skin was smoked, rubbed, washed, and dressed so as to make it soft, dry, and pliant. The skins were folded with the fur inside and tied into bundles or "packs" by means of thongs of green buckskin which dried and shrank to the hardness of iron bands. Some of the posts used wedge presses for this purpose. In spite of the general skill of the Indians in the preparation of furs, as the demands of the trade grew (and as the price of beavers dropped from time to time), packs were not infrequently the repository of occasional heads, feet, tails, etc. This was of no great moment during the cold winter collecting season, when the packs were frozen solid in storage or buried in caches. But they could and did become fetid indeed when they warmed up in the spring! When one considers the primitive curing methods and lack of refrigerated storage and transportation, one marvels at the ability of the French and Indians to carry on such trade at all. Small wonder the traders headed downriver with their packs of furs as soon as the ice broke on the river in the spring.

Aside from the all-important Indians, the personnel in this two-way trading system were divided into three main types. First were the great entrepreneurs—favorites of the crown or the governor usually—who were known as *congés* or *fermiers*. They had grants of major posts or trade territories, or of an entire river in the case of Deruisseau, *congé* at Fort de Cavagnial, or Manuel Lisa during the later period. They were not merchants, but more in the nature of brokers or farmers-out of trade privileges. Since they could not possibly work their territory alone, they in turn granted licenses to lesser *fermiers* or *voyageurs* who actually acquired goods and boats on their own account and sent them to the Indians for trade. They in turn obtained the services of *engagés*, hired boatmen and traders who signed on for a term usually of three years. George Caleb

Fur Traders Descending the Missouri by George Caleb Bingham. Courtesy of the Metropolitan Museum of Art.

Bingham has given us a picturesque view, which appears on the cover of this book, of a French Creole trader descending the Missouri in his wooden pirogue, his half-breed son leaning casually on a pack of furs and a bear cub sitting on the prow. Those fortunate enough to view the original in the Metropolitan Museum in New York will be treated to a newly cleaned original with sparkling colors.

Fur trading was a lonesome, laborious, hazardous occupation. The economics of the calling (and the terms of the *engagé's* contract) served to keep the *engagés* perpetually in debt, so that the fruits from one term's labors were barely sufficient to pay the necessary expenditures for the next. There also was always the danger that the fur seeker would himself become the quarry and his own scalp the peltry sought after. And there could never have been a more fickle or hard to please customer than the Indian. The problems of the traders were aptly summed up by a recent writer on the Missouri fur trade:

The successful trader had to have a thorough knowledge of each tribe with which he dealt, for each had differing needs and desires. One tribe would take a three-point blanket of solid red, while another wanted the same blanket with a blue stripe, and still a third might want only blue two-and-one-half-point blankets. The same was true of beads, although blue ones were universally in demand; knives, mirrors, and even tomahawks, with tribes designating various sizes and weights, some even specifying hammer heads or spikes opposite the blade. This meant that a man planning to trade with very many tribes had to carry a fantastic variety of goods. Not only that, but the trader had to know approximately how much of each article to have on hand for each tribe so as not to be overstocked and have to return with unsalable goods, and yet have enough not to run out and lose a whole trade for want of one article. As a last resort, the trader had to be an excellent salesman, able to convince the natives that the goods he carried they either wanted or needed.

Just as the fur trade and the Chouteaus built St. Louis, so the same combination was responsible for the first permanent large-scale commercial enterprise at Kawsmouth. In a later chapter we will recount the development of the little French Creole community sometimes called Chez les Canses or Chouteau's town and its French-speaking predecessors who farmed and trapped, beginning about 1798, in the area now encompassed by present-day Kansas City.

CHAPTER VI

Lewis & Clark
& Drouillard & Charbonneau

SOME PRELIMINARY OBSERVATIONS may be in order for this chapter lest the author be taken for an out-and-out Francophile. First, the absolutely remarkable achievements of the Lewis and Clark expedition and the benefits they conferred upon the republic are, of course, not questioned in the least. Indeed, they can never be sufficiently praised and memorialized. But this is a story about Frenchmen and Kansas City. It is all too easy to read uncritically the journals and the letters of the Lewis and Clark expedition without ever realizing that what started out as a purely American undertaking metamorphosed into a joint Franco-American enterprise when the exploring party reached French-speaking St. Louis. We (like the young expedition leaders) tend to forget that the nondescript "watermen" and "interpreters" who accompanied the expedition were really intrepid French-Canadians who had their own individualities and skills and culture, however obscure to the Yankee explorers. During the first half of the route, they were merely showing Lewis and Clark what had been their own backyard for over a century. Their countrymen, the LaVendreyes, had explored as far as the northern Rockies, fully two-thirds along the route, as early as 1742. The idea that they were "exploring" country they and their fathers and grandfathers had traversed annually for decades would surely have struck them as a good joke. It is their story which this part of my narrative seeks to tell, predicated on the proposition that they made a vital contribution to the Lewis and Clark expedition, which in turn contributed to the eventual settlement and development of the Kansas City area and the entire Missouri River country.

It will no doubt come as a surprise to many to learn that the explorations conducted by the Lewis and Clark expedition were actually first assigned to, and embarked upon by, a Frenchman. Andre Michaux, a naturalist, was engaged by Thomas Jefferson, in behalf of the American Philosophical Society at Philadelphia in 1793, to "explore the country along the Missouri, and thence westwardly to the Pacific Ocean." Specifically Jefferson instructed him, in the name of the Society, as follows:

> They observe to you that the chief objects of your journey are to find the shortest and most convenient route of communication between the U.S. and the Pacific Ocean, within the temperate latitudes, and to learn such particulars as can be obtained of the country through which it passes, its productions, inhabitants, and other interesting circumstances.
>
> As a channel of communication between these states and the Pacific Ocean, the Missouri, so far as it extends, presents itself under circumstances of unquestioned preference. It has therefore been declared as a fundamental object of the subscription (not to be dispensed with) that this river shall be considered and explored as a part of the communication sought for.

The subscribers to the society's fund included Jefferson and George Washington. Michaux set out upon his journey and got as far as Kentucky, when it was revealed that he was implicated with "Citizen Genet" in a plot by the French to take over Louisiana from the Spanish. This was not the first time the French had dreamed of recovering Louisiana (and with it the future Kansas City) to the fold. Pontiac's War thirty years earlier, in 1764, was probably inspired as much by the Illinois French as by the Indians, and rumor had it that the French military stores placed under Commissary Deruisseau's and Commandant St. Ange's protection in St. Louis in 1764 had been destined for such use. In any event, the scheme of the 1790s died aborning, the plot was revealed, Genet was disgraced, and Michaux was recalled by his government. Other Frenchmen than Michaux were to have the distinction of finding, with Lewis and Clark, the pathway to the Western Sea.

But to return to Lewis and Clark, it will be recalled that the country they were about to explore was in a state of penumbra insofar as sovereignty was concerned. It had been transferred back from Spain to France in 1800. However, the French had never taken back actual military control. Even the Spanish "possession" which existed since 1763 had never been more than nominal in upper Louisiana, and the country remained as it had for well over 100 years, essentially a French-Canadian province. It was so French, indeed, that Lewis and Clark were provided with a French passport to enter their own country's new domain!

The French-speaking community of St. Louis became the advance base for the Lewis and Clark expedition. It was the last major entrepôt on the route to the West—the jumping-off point where reliable military and commercial transportation and mail from the East ended. Just how dependent the expedition was on the French can be seen from the fact that they had to rely upon the French *voyageurs* to provide their line of communication—they were Lewis and Clark's postal system. Also, the principal map of the proposed route of the expedition was compiled from information supplied by the French St. Louis inhabitants.

Captain Lewis seems also to have relied heavily for background information upon a French engineer-historian, LePage Du Pratz and his *Histoire de La Louisiane*, an English translation of which Lewis carried with him on the trip. In St. Louis, Lewis recruited a group of "watermen"—i.e., Frenchmen who were skilled in handling craft on the Missouri River. Their abilities were almost indispensable in order to convey such a sizable party and their impedimenta up the hazardous river to the Mandan villages. Most of them (the French) traveled in the "red pirogue" as *engagés* under Patron (Captain) Baptiste Deschamps, and their names were Etienne Mabbauf, Paul Primaut, Charle Hebert, Baptiste La Jeunesse, Peter Pinaut, Peter Roi, and Joseph Collin. These men were engaged only for the trip to the Mandans and were not military enlistees— however, a few French names (Bruyott, Labich, LePage) are also apparent in the troop lists of the expedition. One Frenchman reported to have made the entire trip was La Liberte, who later settled in the French community which became Kansas City and whose name is listed on an 1840 map of the village (written in French). To this list of Frenchmen must be added the French-Canadian interpreters George Drouillard and Toussaint Charbonneau—undoubtedly the most—and least—useful, respectively, of the Frenchmen accompanying the expedition.

Drouillard, son of a French-Canadian father and a Shawnee mother, a resident of the Cape Girardeau district, was unquestionably the most important member of the expedition after the two commandants. He was the highest paid of all the other men, made the entire trip to the Pacific and back, and at times seems to have even shared command responsibilities with (or was delegated the same by) the expedition leaders. His biographer rightfully comments that:

> But for the efforts and accomplishments of this man it is certain the Lewis and Clark expedition would not have attained the success acclaimed for it today.

In addition to his official capacity as "interpreter," he was the invaluable chief hunter and provisioner (for 45-50 men), boat steerer, diplomatic negotiator with the Indians, trusted confidant of Captain Lewis and his deputy in the apprehension of deserters, and (with Sacajawea) the acquirer of indispensable horses from the Shoshones to enable the expedition to cross the Continental Divide and thus achieve its mission.

Of Drouillard, Lewis said in his report to the Secretary of War that he was:

> A man of much merit; he has been peculiarly useful from his knowledge of the common language of gesticulation, and his uncommon skill as a hunter and woodsman; those several duties he performed in good faith, and with an order which deserves the highest commendation. It was also his fate to have encountered, on various occasions with either Captain Clark or myself, all the most dangerous and trying scenes of the voyage, in which he uniformly acquitted himself with honor.

Two other Frenchmen were of great assistance to the expedition. The editor of the Lewis and Clark correspondence notes that "Rene Auguste Chouteau (1749-1829) fur trader and merchant and his brother Jean Pierre proved indispensable to Lewis and Clark in many ways." Prior to setting out, Lewis and Clark spent much of the winter of 1803-1804 in Pierre Chouteau's home at St. Louis. During this period they were engaged in collecting supplies and personnel for their journey, to which endeavors the French made a major contribution. Auguste's and Pierre's homes were the mansions of St. Louis of that day, with two and one-half stories and 60 foot fronts (probably eighty counting their magnificent galleries or porches all around). Many were the fetes and *bals* given by the French for the young commandants that winter in St. Louis. Pierre acted as agent for Captain Lewis at St. Louis under his power of attorney while the expedition was en route, and President Jefferson referred to him as "our Indian agent at St. Louis."

Charbonneau bears further mention. Toussaint Charbonneau was everyone's idea of a bush-ranger—shiftless, unreliable, slovenly, impecunious—whereas his Shoshone Indian

wife, Sacajawea, was almost the embodiment of Chateau-
briand's romanticized version of the "noble savage." Charbonneau, the interpreter hired before leaving winter camp
with the Mandan Sioux, was to prove a source of constant
irritation to the expedition's leaders (including the more
responsible among the French contingent). But his highly
intelligent and diplomatic wife really saved the expedition
when she bargained for absolutely indispensable horses from
the Shoshone Indians in order to make the arduous trek over
the Continental Divide. Kidnapped as a girl by an enemy
tribe, she was sold to the Mandans, who had sold her to
Charbonneau. Lewis and Clark quickly realized the advantages to be gained by repatriating her (which, in the event, she
declined). It was actually her brother who saved the expedition
by supplying horses in a transport of joy when seeing his sister
again. She carried her infant son, Jean-Baptiste, throughout
the remainder of the expedition, and he is reported to have
later settled for a time in the Kansas City area.

It can readily be seen that whatever benefits may have been
conferred by the expedition upon the Kansas City area (and
there were many), they were greatly furthered by Frenchmen,
many of whom had been to our area before. So well-traveled
was this watercourse, in fact, that most of the place names
mentioned by Lewis and Clark in the Kansas City vicinity
were long-established French names familiar to the Frenchmen and recited by them to the leaders as they went along. On
the Clay County side above the Little Blue were Charretins
(Otter) Creeks. On the Jackson County side were La Char-
bonniere (Coal) Creek and La Benite (Consecrated?) Creek.
Above the Kansas were Petite Riviere Platte (Shoal), Bisquit
Creek and Remore (Tree Frog) Creek, Isle des Parques (Field
Islands, near Leavenworth), Parques Creek, and Isle au Vache
(Cow Island.) The Blue River was referred to as the Blue
Water Creek, and it originated as the French *L'Eau d'Azur*.

Not only had the French named the rivers, creeks, and
islands in our area, they or their French-Indian relatives had

also built habitations here. The expedition on Sunday, June 24, 1804, passed "Hay Cabin Creek" (now the Little Blue) "so called from camps of straw built on it." The "Hay Cabins" give a tenuous, but reasonably arguable, claim to an eighteenth century date for the first semi-permanent habitations constructed in the metropolitan Kansas City area (albeit by the Indians, but accompanied by their French traders) and for the commencement of regular commercial enterprise here. This is not to deprecate Avion who located on the Kansas side in 1752 (trying to divert trade from Fort de Cavagnial), but he stayed only a brief period, and we know of no permanent structures erected by him. The expedition seems not to have found anyone living right at or near Kawsmouth, although they and their French *engagés* constructed here "a strong redoubt or brest work from one river to the other, of logs and bushes six feet high." They named it "Camp Mouth of the Kansies" and stayed in it for about three days. It must not be assumed that the region was deserted, in spite of the lack of reports of permanent settlement. There may well have been French squatters at that early date at Randolph Bluffs, three miles below present Kansas City, and on the north bank of the river opposite present River Quay, and in the old French Bottoms in what is now the Kansas City Central Industrial District. There are several reliable later references to these early farmers, but it would be useless to speculate on why Lewis and Clark did not mention them. An indigenous population is somewhat an embarrassment to "trailblazers." The expedition met as many as one trader a day on the lower Missouri, including one coming from up the Kansas River with his furs on a raft made of two canoes lashed together.

Just above Leavenworth (and still within the periphery of the metropolitan Kansas City area) the party examined the remains of old Fort de Cavagnial. As noted previously, the Lewis and Clark party found the location of the old fort which was still identifiable by the outlines of the fortification, the remains of chimneys, and the old spring which had supplied the fort. Since the Kansa had stayed on for some years at their village of 12 (i.e., 12 French leagues above the Kansas River), it is possible that French traders had kept some of the abandoned fort's cabins in habitable shape for a time beyond 1764. One of the Frenchmen in the party was well enough acquainted with the occupation of the fort to tell Captain Lewis that when the French were there they kept their horses and cattle on the islands (Parque Islands and possibly Kickapoo and Isle au Vache) in the river. Just above Isle au Vache (visible from the village of 12) they landed at "an old trading house" on the south side. The journals note that "a beautiful small run passes back of the trading house near the high land." This trading house may have been made of logs, since one of grass thatch would have seemingly been referred to in the same manner as the "hay cabins." It was unequivocally said to be "old." Here again, therefore, we apparently have evidence of fairly permanent eighteenth century occupation by French fur traders not far from the Kansas City metropolitan area.

When Lewis and Clark journeyed up the Missouri River, they passed the vicinity of Wolf River in Doniphan County, Kansas, on July 9, 1804. Sergeant Floyd wrote in his journal (no doubt relying on eyewitness accounts from the French boatmen in the party) of the former presence on the south (west) bank of the Missouri, slightly below Wolf River, of a settlement of "several French families" who were there "some years ago." He noted further that they stayed for two years and raised corn during that time, and that the Indians were very friendly. These were probably the French-speaking Kansa who had never really been out of contact with the French since the abandonment of Fort de Cavagnial. Capt. William Clark said his French "bowman" told him of the little colony, where some "cabins" still stood and said he had lived there a few years before. Bliss Iseley, a noted Kansas historian, has written that these French farmers were from St. Charles, on the Missouri River northwest of present St. Louis, Missouri, and that their settlement existed from 1795 to 1796.

We know that at the time the Lewis and Clark expedition commenced the Chouteaus held one of the last licenses to trade with the Kansa, and they perhaps continued to use it actively as long as they could. But French trade in the future Kansas City area was interrupted for a few years (over the violent and eventually successful objection of the French-Americans) by the establishment of Jefferson's system of trading "factories," including Fort Clark (Osage). The commanding site for the fort was apparently selected by Lewis and Clark as they passed it during the expedition. Opening the area to commerce was a major purpose of the expedition. The establishment of this fort probably inhibited permanent French-American settlement at Kansas City for some years, since private trading was temporarily abolished and the Kansa were required to trade at the fort. Whatever plans, if any, the Chouteaus may have had for setting up a trading emporium at Kawsmouth had to mark time while the fort was there.

When Jefferson told the Kansa and Osage about plans for the government trading post, their reply reveals to us the then (January 1806) state of commercial integrity of the French-speaking traders in the Kawsmouth area:

> Fathers, we believe that you wish to pity us and prevent our wants by sending us supplies of goods, but look sharp and tell your men to take not too much fur for a little of goods, should they act in that way we would not be better off than we are now with our actual [i.e., French] traders.

With the interested reader who has gotten this far, I would like to share my discovery of Anna Lee Waldo's *Sacajawea*, published in both pocket and hardcover form. Would that a sequel could be done on this magnificent woman's son, Jean Baptiste Charbonneau, premiere guide of the west.

After the Lewis and Clark expedition, George Drouillard worked briefly for Manuel Lisa in the upper Missouri trade, was tried ignominiously for killing a man (albeit in the line of duty), and was sometime later decapitated and eaten by the

Blackfoot Indians in 1810 within sight of Fort Mandan, only a few years after his Lewis and Clark exploits.

Charbonneau, on the other hand, lived for more than eighty-one winters. He showed up with a new young squaw bride nearly every other year (including his eightieth, when he was given a grand shivaree by the traders at Fort Mandan); survived the War of 1812 in the West (when he served the American cause well by keeping the friendship of the Missouri Indians from swinging to the British); worked for Manuel Lisa, was imprisoned in Santa Fe; then guided for the Long expedition for Prince Paul of Wurttemberg and for Maximilian Prince of Wied; and spent his remaining years living as an Indian with the Mandans on a government interpreter's stipend. He died survived by several children, including a son, Jean Baptiste (by his famous wife Sacajawea). His son had been given a parochial school education in St. Louis by Capt. William Clark, adopted as a protegé by Prince Paul of Wurttemberg in Europe, received a classical education, and became a legendary guide for the famous in the American West! In fact there are Charbonneaus all over Kansas and the Midwest, mostly descendants of his numerous progeny. The race is not always to the swift!

CHAPTER VII

The Kansas Cajuns

NOW WE MOVE TO THE western periphery of the Kansas City metropolitan area in order to discuss some highly interesting French-speaking expatriates originally from the Kansa village north of Kansas City—the so-called "Kansas Half-Breeds." This grossly ethnic term was thrust upon us by the usage of 1825, when a somewhat conscience-stricken government set aside certain lands in order to compensate these more civilized (i.e., more European), evicted former residents of the Kansas City area. I prefer to call them the "French-Kansa." These were the French-speaking members of the Kansa Indian tribe who also could claim progenitors who, in the aggregate, were sufficient to constitute them approximately 50 percent or more descended from French stock. Many were nearly full-blooded French and contemporary writers so described them. Some of their family lines may have run all the way back to Louis XIV's military and trade expedition under Bourgmont in 1714 and certainly back to the 20-year occupation of Fort de Cavagnial in 1744-1764, and later traders. Just as the Acadians (the French Cajuns who were removed, like Longfellow's Evangeline, against their will by the British in 1755), the French-Kansa in 1825 were compelled to move from their homes in eastern Kansas. For some of the French-Kansa descendants of Louisiana traders, it may have been the second time around, since some of the Cajuns from Louisiana had (like Evangeline's Gabriel) drifted up the Mississippi and Missouri in the later 1700s and entered the fur trade.

The descriptions of the French-Kansa, while not altogether flattering, are nevertheless interesting to those who wish to trace the history of the French in our area. The most definitive treatment to date of the Kansa Indians describes them as having "a powerful French influence as part of their tribal tradition." The Reverend Smith, investigating the possibility of a Presbyterian mission among the Kansa in 1833, wrote that "the most of them are low French, and half-breeds, some tainted with infidelity and some with papacy." Allowing for what we might now call Reverend Smith's WASP bias, what was happening was the disintegration of an erstwhile Catholic Gallic-Indian culture whose French supporters had lost out politically, militarily, and economically, and whose Kansa Indian relatives were all being removed at musket-point to the West. The fines trapped in the government sieve after these other two groups were strained out were the French-Kansa— neither fish nor fowl—not Indian enough to go to the reservation, and yet not wholly French.

Many of the French-Kansa were sensitive, articulate, intelligent people who eventually contributed, by themselves or through their progeny, to the betterment of their state and nation. Their world was falling apart in 1825, and they were being told to give up their ancestral homes and hunting grounds, which they loved, and take up farming, which they hated, while their Indian cousins and lifelong friends were herded off to the new Kansa reservation in central and western Kansas. The French-Kansa were by far the most civilized element of the Kansa nation and felt it only their due that they should receive some recompense for being uprooted from their (then) Kansas River homes. White Plume, the principal Kansa chief, a handsome man of commanding presence, was a highly intelligent, well-traveled, and surprisingly articulate spokesman for them. Indeed, he told the authorities they should build him a substantial stone house befitting his station in life (they did in 1827). He was instrumental in obtaining a French-speaking Catholic priest by the name of Father Lutz

Portrait of Kansa Chief White Plume by Charles Bird King. Courtesy of Kansas State Historical Society.

who ministered briefly to the Kansa, as is noted later.

The Kansas Cajuns, like the real Acadians in Louisiana (many of them also half-breeds), even had their "Evangelines"—four of them, in fact. White Plume's French-speaking granddaughters (Josette, Julie, Pelagie, and Victoire Gonville) were used to the good life and the edifying company of their prominent grandfather and their French father, Louis Gonville, an interpreter and trader. Josette (Mary Josephine) had, in fact, been raised at the Kansas City home of François and Berenice Chouteau. The similarity of the two stories, Evangeline's and that of the Gonville sisters, is interesting. Perhaps they eventually read "Evangeline" and noted the poignant similarities themselves since Longfellow published his poem in 1847. The basic plot is, of course, the same—the displacement of an indigenous French-speaking Catholic population by English-speaking Protestant outsiders. But, the similarity does not stop there. The Gonville sisters were French Catholics all, each, mayhap, like Evangeline with her "chaplet of beads and her missal." For a short while, they even had the services (but not in an actual church) of a French-speaking Catholic priest, Fr. Joseph Anthony Lutz, a missionary from the Diocese of St. Louis. Of each of them, perhaps it could be said, with Longfellow:

> Fair was she to behold, that maid of seventeen summers.
> Black were her eyes as the berry that grows on the thorn by the
>   wayside,
> Black, yet how softly they gleamed beneath the brown shade of her
>   tresses,
> . . .
> Fairer was she when, on Sunday morn, while the bell from its turret
> Sprinkled with holy sounds the air, as the priest with his hyssop
> Sprinkles the congregation, and scatters blessings upon them.

We know, however, that Josette was only eight years old at the time of the 1825 removal. Their grandfather and father had been the most influential men in their village (like Evangeline's father, Benedict Bellefontaine), and they had enjoyed, like she, more of the amenities than their peers. Their fiances, like Evangeline's Gabriel, were *voyageurs* in the fur trade, dealing in beaver and bison and other furs, not far from the Ozarks. (But they were luckier—Josette, Pelagie, and Victoire each married their affianced, three brothers who were the sons of Louis Pappan, a prominent St. Louis fur jobber with interests among the Kansa and Osage.) All this was shattered by the removal order, and well could they relate to Longfellow's soliloquy delivered by the officer who addressed the assembled Acadians on the fateful day in 1755:

> *. . . all your lands, and dwellings, and cattle of all kinds*
> *Forfeited be to the crown; and that you yourselves from this province*
> *Be transported to other lands. God grant you may*
> *Ever as faithful subjects, a happy and peaceable people dwell there!*

Just as in the notes to Longfellow's Acadian poem, "Parents were separated from children and husbands from wives, some of whom have not met to this day again." In the case of the French-Kansa, however, this separation was brought about not so much by actual force, but rather by the force of circumstances which dictated whether one went to the Kansas prairies (the full-bloods), Kansas City, St. Louis, New Orleans, or to the mountains (the French fathers), or whether one made do on the "half-breed" lands in Kansas (the young French-Kansa brothers and sisters whose fathers were the French *voyageurs*).

Josette, Julie, Pelagie, and Victoire Gonville were each theoretically allotted an entire section of land as recompense for the expropriation of their homeland, as were Marie and Lafleche Gonville, who were apparently cousins (daughters of Baptiste Gonville). The lands given to these French-speaking Kansa consisted of a row of 23 whole sections of land extending roughly from north of Topeka (lot 4 was just north of Topeka) easterly to lot 23 north of Lecompton (near Lawrence). This was excellent river-bottom (and partially forested). The French names of the grantees are redolent of their paternal lineage in Normandy and Languedoc, and perhaps are of some interest.

They were (reading from west to east):

> *Lot No. Name*
> 1   Adele Lessert Belmare (Bellemarde)

2	Clement Lessert, Jr.
3	Josette Gonville Pappan (Papin)
4	Julie Gonville Pappan
5	Pelagie Gonville Pappan
6	Victoire Gonville
7	Marie Gonville
8	Lafleche Gonville
9	Louis Laventure
10	Elizabeth Carbonau
11	Pierre Carbonau
12	Louis Joncas
13	Basil Joncas
14	James Joncas
15	Elizabeth Datcherute
16	Joseph Butler
17	William Rodgers
18	Joseph Cote
19-22	Compare, fils
23	Joseph James

White Plume (sometimes called White Feather), while a full-blooded Kansa, had the heart, mind, and tongue of a Frenchman. Fr. Nicolas Point, Catholic priest at Kawsmouth who met White Plume, said he was "endowed with an intelligence, a sincerity, and a courage not of the usual kind." The most famous picture of him shows him in Indian dress with his Lewis and Clark medallion on his chest. The reverse of the medallion shows an American uniformed officer shaking hands with a *French* uniformed person below a crossed calumet and tomahawk—clearly indicating that the other party was a grand chief of a friendly tribe in his French officer's uniform. (It is worth remembering that Lewis and Clark carried a *French* passport when they left St. Louis!) Chief Pontiac had worn his complete dress uniform, given to him by General Montcalm, in St. Louis shortly before his death. Perhaps White Plume, too, had such a uniform for special occasions.

In addition to White Plume, we have information about a number of the other progenitors of the 23 grantees of the French-Kansa sections. Clement Lessert, father of Adele (Tract 1) and Clement, Jr. (Tract 2), was the official interpreter for the Kansa nation, lived in Chouteau's or Chez les Canses (probably Lot 2 on Father Point's 1840 map) and was an "old friend" of William Mulkey, an early settler. Louis Gonville, White Plume's son-in-law and father of Josette (Tract 3), Julie (Tract 4), Pelagie (Tract 5), and Victoire (Tract 6), was a French interpreter and trader with the Kansa. Baptiste Gonville, father of Marie (Tract 7) and Lafleche (Tract 8), another French trader, was Louis Gonville's brother. "Laventure" (Tract 9) was Louis Laventure, son of another French trader, Francis Laventure. Toussaint Charbonneau (of Sacajawea fame) had a daughter named Lizette, possibly by his famous wife, who was raised as the ward of Gen. William Clark in St. Louis. She may have been Elizabeth Carbonau (Tract 10) whose brother was presumably Pierre Carbonau (Tract 11). Charbonneau was French interpreter for some Kansa traders in 1823, which could help to explain why French-Shoshone children were given Kansa lands. Their father is listed as Pierre Brisa (not Carbonau) which suggests perhaps an adoptive father who lodged them with the Kansa. A "Carboneau" had lot No. 4 on Father Point's 1840 Kansas City map. Lizette married Vertifeuille (of Lot 7 on Father Point's map) and her daughter Victoire was baptized in 1843. Baptiste Datcherute, father of Elizabeth Datcherute (Tract 15), was an incumbent Kansa interpreter when the treaty of 1825 ceding the Kansa lands was signed, and he was one of the official witnesses to the treaty conveying a section of land to his daughter. Of Joncas, Butler, Rodgers, Cote, Compare, and James nothing more is known to the writer at present.

Interestingly, these quasi-Frenchmen apparently preferred to raise dollars rather than crops, since the Indian superintendent at St. Louis reported in 1840 that most of them were living in St. Louis, where they repeatedly besieged his office for permission to sell their lands along the Kansas River. Like Evangeline, the Kansas Cajuns had gravitated toward their French cousins elsewhere, unable to return to the ancestral lands from which they had been banished. Still another indignity awaited them, however. Squatters had settled on their newly allotted lands, and when they tried to sell them to financially responsible buyers, they discovered the enabling legislation and treaty allowed the full-blood Kansa to sell their common lands but didn't provide for sales by the half-breeds of their own lots! Pelagie and Victoire spent a good part of their lives trying to obtain justice in the granting of their patrimony, and after many years won a Pyrrhic victory in the U.S. Supreme Court on this point—but by then it was 1870 and many of the original French-Kansa were dead! Indeed, not until 1968 did Congress pay the 400 heirs of the French-Kansa the appraised valuation (as of 1862) of $5.00 per acre, and as late as 1970 claims were still pending for millions of dollars of interest remaining unpaid on the 1862 appraised value. *Malheureusement*, the descendants of the French-Kansa are still suffering their tribulations. In the case of *Tommy Joe Dennison* (a descendant of Adele Lessert Bellemere or Bell-marde, grantee of Tract No. 1) vs. *Topeka Chambers Industrial Development*, No. 79-1668, a class action on behalf of the 400 descendants of the original 23 grantees filed in 1983 in the U.S. District Court for Kansas at Wichita and appealed after an adverse judgment to the Tenth Circuit at Denver, the claimants again in January, 1984 lost, apparently forever, their ancestral rights to their lands north of Topeka. The case will be a reported decision of the Tenth Circuit U.S. Court of Appeals. Incredible as it may seem, some of the fathers and spouses of these unfortunate and much-abused grantees were of the wealthy and influential French mercantile aristocratic families in St. Louis and Kansas City! Pelagie's and Victoire's long trek seems to have come to naught. Longfellow's description of Evangeline's lifelong struggle is apt here:

Fair was she and young, when in hope began the long
    journey;
Faded was she and old, when in disappointment it ended.

A letter from the Kansa Indian agent to the Superintendent of Indian Affairs at St. Louis, dated October 1, 1856, while after the close of the main drama of this book, speaks volumes about what became of the French-Kansa's lands (on which some of them were still trying to remain in possession for "many years after 1862"):

Sir: It seems that the affairs and present condition of this agency should attract more than the usual attention of those whose duty and whose business it is to exercise a supervision for the present interest and future welfare of those people, whose rights, established by treaty and by law, have been encroached, but who have remained remarkably quiet and unobtrusive, refraining from any infringement or violation of their sacred treaties with the government, relying upon those in whom they never fail to repose the greatest confidence for that protection of their rights, their land and property, which is justly due them. . . .

The tract of country on the north side of the Kansas River known as the half-breed Kansas reservation, has for the last two years been the object of filthy speculation. . . . [T]he lower portion of the reservation . . . has been, and is at this time, subject to the intrusion of lawless men; stripping the land of its timber, opening farms, cultivating the soil, and appropriating the fruits to their own use. . . .

The larger portion of the half-breed Kansas reserve now quietly rests in the possession of the intruders, after actually driving by force and violence from one or two of the tracts the identical Indians for whom the land was reserved. . . .

The half-breed Kansas, or the greater number of them, are industrious and intelligent, well-versed in the English, French and Kaw languages, profess the Catholic religion, and have almost a thorough knowledge of the arts of

Drawing of St. Francis Regis Church by Fr. Nicholas Point.

husbandry. . . . The Canadian French, in my opinion, have done more to civilize the Kansas than all the schools and moral institutions that have ever been established for their benefit.

Contrast this last statement with the previously mentioned report of the Protestant missionary group's agent that the intelligent and devout Gonville sisters and their peers were "low (i.e., part Indian) French" and "infected with Papacy"!

The Kansa Indian agent's favorable comment echoes that of Fr. Nicholas Point, curé to the little French village at Kawsmouth a few years later:

I can affirm that if the harvest already reaped cost us efforts, even though consoling, it is, after God, to the French that we are indebted. And, if not to the French of France, then at least to their descendants or to the Indians converted by French missionaries. These *voyageurs*, whom Providence scattered throughout these regions, did not, it is true, always conduct themselves in conformity with their faith, but none of them took it upon himself to speak disrespectfully either of his religion, or the priests, or of his country. And since there were those among them who spoke of these things only with the most respectful affection, it was impossible for their sentiments not to be communicated in some measure to their hosts.

Are the French-Kansa still in the Topeka/Kansas City area? Perhaps some are still there. Moyse Bellemere and Adele Lessert moved to Reserve No. 2 in 1841 according to Barry's *Annals of Kansas*, and Joseph Papin and Josette Gonville moved to Josette's Reserve No. 3 in 1840. The Papins operated the Kaw River ferry at Topeka for years, from Reserve No. 4 in north Topeka. There are listings for Papin (Pappan) and Cote in the current Topeka (and Kansas City) telephone directory. Julie Pappan's grandson, Charles Curtis, lived as a boy on Reserve No. 4 with his French-speaking grandmother and grew up to become Vice-President of the United States. Clement Lessert, Pierre and Elizabeth Carbonau (Carbonere), and Adele Bellemarde (Belmare) lived in Kansas City in later years and were parishioners of the French St. Francis Regis ("Chouteau's") Church. Josette Gonville married Joseph Papin at Chouteau's church in present Kansas City on October 25, 1837. The real estate records for the French-Kansa strip of land still showed some of the old French names until not too many years ago, and "Papin" or "Pappan" is a familiar name to area title examiners. Bliss Isley said there is "much French blood in Kansas." But their command of French is long dimmed, and the colorful ways of their ancestors are not the ways of today. The old home of the French-Kansa is no more.

Still stands the forest primeval; but under the shade of its branches
Dwells another race, with other customs and language.

CHAPTER VIII

Creole Kansas City: A Potpourri

CREOLE MAY SEEM a characterization totally foreign—even offensive—to apply to the early-day residents of the French enclave which became Kansas City. But Creoles they were, as all the writers of that time attest, and it helps to understand why the term was used and what it meant. It was a term of description, not opprobrium. No less a personage than Prince Paul of Wurttemberg visited the French community near Kawsmouth on June 21, 1823, and described it as a "little settlement of Creoles and half-breeds."

How Creoles in Kansas City? Of course, it wasn't Kansas then, it was Chez les Canses or Kanzas, and it was made up of Frenchmen from Canada and from New Orleans—trappers from the bayou country of Louisiana. Kansas City is, after all, on a Mississippi tributary just 700 feet above the elevation of New Orleans (which was, in those days, the next stop after St. Louis). The nearest bayou, indeed, is Illinois Bayou just 55 miles south of the Missouri border in Arkansas. Creole was not a term of denigration. It referred to persons of French descent born in Louisiana, with or without the admixture of other nationalities. The best description of the life-style of the Creoles is that given by a very thorough student of the West, Hiram Crittenden in his *American Fur Trade of the Far West.* In that study Crittenden said:

But the Creoles of the North and South bore little enough resemblance to the same generations of Frenchmen in the motherland. The rapid progress of France in the disturbing ideas of the times, which culminated in the Revolution, was not shared by the colonists in the new world; and the settlements in the far interior of America were more like the French village of the time of Louis XIV than those of the period in which they actually flourished. . . . They loved the quiet, listless ways of their fathers. The enterprising spirit of the Anglo-Saxon had no charms for them, honest and punctilious in their dealings, courts and lawyers were almost unknown. Crime was very rare and jails were not found necessary. Wealth and beggary were alike absent. Ambition was not a trait of their character. Art and learning had not taken root. Even the commonest manufactures seem to have been lacking and the people derived their living from the field and from the chase. But with all this apparent lack of the qualities which seem to us essential to the growth of any community, they were a happy people. They were fond of amusements, in which the celebration of the church fetes bore a prominent part. They were unselfish, hospitable and friendly in their intercourse. . . . On the whole they represented a type of life over which the contemplative mind delights to linger, and it is a doubtful question whether in its extinction the world has not lost something which the present substitute does not adequately replace.

The makeup of the little French community which was Kansas City in the early 1800s ranged all the way from the aristocratic and wealthy Chouteaus (and Menards) with their old-world graces and connections, to the Creole *voyageurs* who were, as one visitor put it "principally engaged in producing half-breeds." Madame Montardeau (Montardy), a resident, was "an educated woman who before the days of the French Revolution was a student in one of the best convent academies in her native France. Her parents were killed by the [revolutionaries] and her property confiscated." The inventories of the estates of families such as the Chouteaus, Menards, etc. in

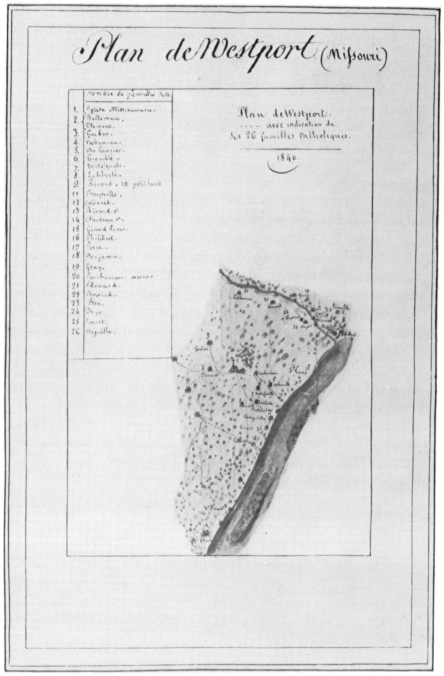

"Plan de Westport" by Fr. Nicholas Point.

St. Louis and Kaskaskia were almost incredible for that day and place: whole sets of the classics and fashions right out of the Paris salons! Fortunately, there is a map still extant, drawn by Father Nicolas Point in 1840 entitled "Plan de Westport," which shows the names of the two dozen or so French residents and the location of their homes on the river banks (Kaw or Missouri). There were actually quite a number of additional residents from time to time, but they were single men who either were off in the mountains on Chouteau's fur business or bunked in the Chouteau warehouse/store. We know that those of the French who lived near the Kaw in an area long known as the French Bottoms (where the Central Industrial District is now located) felled trees (the area was then heavily forested) and cleared little strips of land running back inland from the river. These were in all probability rough equivalents of the arpent strips almost universally used by the French in their various settlements, including St. Louis, St. Charles, and Ste. Genevieve. They were based on the "Paris acre" which was 192½ English feet wide and quite long, running (in St. Louis) as many as 40 arpents back from the river. Original entry upon this land was governed (albeit rather casually) by the St. Louis/St. Charles Spanish authorities, and there were some later formal dealings in these tracts. These strip tracts are the subject of an amusing story told of two of the old Kansas City French residents.

> It seems that Louis Tremble and Benjamin Legautherie decided to exchange their tracts of land and actually moved into each other's cabins. But when it came to the execution of the deed, Madame Tremble refused to sign her mark unless, according to an old custom, she was given a new silk gown. The two tracts together did not equal the value of a silk gown, so the deeds were torn up and they moved back to their original cabins.

Since *Legautherie* is one of the several (mis)spellings of *La Gautrais,* Benjamin may have been a son or grandson of Pierre

Rene Harpin de la Gautrais, the engineer who selected the site of Fort de Cavagnial, and who still had property in the St. Louis area in the late 1770s (having moved his residence to New Orleans).

A dowry, given by the father of the bride, was very much a part of the French Creole social milieu in early-day Kansas City. Another amusing anecdote is told of a fairly well-to-do old landholder, who let it be known that a substantial tract of land would accompany his daughter in marriage. To his surprise, a highly undesirable suitor, after a whirlwind courtship, successfully wooed and wed his daughter. He kept his word to give a dowry of land, but gave the groom a virtually useless (in those agrarian days) long thin strip only 19 rods, or about 1½ arpents, wide. It now comprises some of the most valuable real estate in Kansas City, fronting along midtown Broadway!

The French Creoles were a hardy lot. Fr. Bernard Donnelly, an early-day Catholic priest here and avid chronicler of the French, told the story of his visit to the old log cabin of one of them, opposite Fifth and Bluff Streets. A newspaper account states:

> The cabin was occupied at the time mentioned (1847) by an old French Creole woman named Madame Grandlouis, then about 70 years of age. Fr. Donnelly . . . visited her and from her learned the story of her first coming to Jackson County, nearly fifty years before, which must have been about 1798 or 1800. . . . She was a native of the French settlement of St. Charles. . . .
>
> Madame Grandlouis described Jackson County at that period as the home and hunting grounds of the Kaw Indians, who claimed exclusive right and jurisdiction over the country now incorporated in Lafayette, Cass, Johnson, and Jackson counties. Their villages were located on the Little Blue which, on account of the high, rank grass found in its bottom lands, and which they used to cover their

teepees or wigwams, they called Cabin Grass Creek. [The French called it "Hay Cabin Creek" for the same reason.] The country then abounded in elk, deer, bear, catamount, wolves, geese, grouse, turkeys and other small game.

The newspaper narrative of Father Donnelly's interview then noted that during the first winter the Missouri froze over, and that:

> One day, during the absence of her husband and his companions, Madame Grandlouis observed a large black bear approaching the cabin. It was walking directly towards her, across the ice . . . and had reached near the centre of the river, when it paused and sat down upon the ice, and proceeded to lick its paws. . . . Madame Grandlouis, young and athletic as a fawn, rifle in hand, started forth from the cabin to meet the dangerous visitor . . . concealed from the unsuspecting bruin, she took aim and fired and killed the monster instantly. This, said Madam Grandlouis, was no unusual occurrence in those days, as both men and women were equally proficient with the rifle.

The article concludes with the observation that Madame Grandlouis lived to be nearly 100 years old and that she was buried in the old French Catholic cemetery on Pennsylvania Avenue (since removed to St. Mary's Cemetery).

Other rather noteworthy residents of Creole Kansas City were mentioned by Prince Paul of Wurttemberg in 1823. He first mentioned the wife of Mr. Woods, a trader whose store had been one of the prime reasons for the Chouteaus' founding of Kansas City. Of her, the Prince said: "She was a Creole, a daughter of old Mr. Chauvin of St. Charles. The whole population of this little settlement consists of only a few persons, Creoles and half-breeds, whose occupation is the trade with the Kansa Indians, some hunting and agriculture. Here I also found a youth of sixteen years of age (Baptiste Charbonneau) whose mother (Sacajawea) had accompanied the

Messrs. Lewis and Clark, as an interpreter, to the Pacific Ocean in 1804-1806. This Indian woman married the French interpreter, Toussaint Charbonneau." The prince befriended young Baptiste, a precocious lad, and took him to Europe with him and gave him an education, later bringing him back on a second trip to the West.

Creole Kansas City possessed a genuine "character" in the person of Jacques Fournais, dit (called) "Old Pino." We shall let Father Donnelly tell his story, slightly revising his order:

> Among those good simple people, the French of Kansas City, I noticed a very old-looking man of singular appearance. His hair was copious and of a silvery whiteness on his head, eyebrows and throat. His face was of a pale whiteness, jaws rather heavy and blue lugubrious eyes; shoulders somewhat bent, apparently by age; but that which attracted my notice in particular was his curious manner of locomotion. His two knees seemed to be always at variance with each other. . . .
>
> For a long time I was under the impression that Pino's deformity of legs was natural to him; and only after a quarter of a century's acquaintance did I discover that it had been caused by one of the most fearful accidents I ever heard of.
>
> He never failed to come to me on every Easter. . . for more than a quarter of a century to prepare himself "pour faire la paques." In the summer of 1846 on a Sunday I noticed that Pino was unusually excited and happy looking. . . . Approaching with a smile all over his face, he informed me that "notre petite Catherine" was just home on vacation from the Sisters of St. Joseph convent at Carondelet. "Voila," said the affectionate old hunter, pointing towards a little half-breed, rosy-cheeked girl about thirteen years of age. I subsequently learned that she was the daughter of Major Dripps and his wife, who was an Otoe Indian (said to be an Indian princess).

An old hunter informed me that Old Pino was in the habit of telling his fellow hunters how terrible was the cannonade on the day when the city of Montreal was taken from the French by the British army. He was then with his father a few miles outside the city, assisting in splitting fence rails.

Some years ago, on a certain day, Old Pino called at my room. He was more than usually conversable. His apparent sociableness might have been imputable to "un petit gout de whiskey" which I suspected had been taken. It occurred to me on the occasion to question him regarding his place of nativity, etc., and his answer was—I distinctly recollect it—"I was born in Montreal, Canada, shortly after the great war [la guerre grande]. I came to Fort Duquesne [Pittsburgh] where I worked around until the following spring and then took a flatboat on the Ohio and Mississippi to New Orleans and, after some time, to St. Louis. [He must have come to Kansas City around 1821.]

On one occasion Pino had set his traps in one of the streams of the Black Hills. Retiring from the spot some distance, he descried a large male buffalo grazing alone on the open prairie. Crawling around, he took steady aim and fired. When the wounded buffalo reached the prostrate form of poor Pino he commenced a savage dance upon his back and head and limbs.

The buffalo, after eyeing Pino for what seemed an eternity, died of Pino's one shot. Pino's leg was broken, and he splinted it with a sapling and dragged himself (nearly one mile a day for 22 days) to reach his companions! His leg bothered him the rest of his life.

Old Pino died in the arms of his "petite Catherine" in the apple orchard behind another settler's house in 1871. An editor's note accompanying the foregoing reprint of Father Donnelly's remarks in the Westport Historical *Quarterly* states that:

Jacques Fournais died in July, 1871, at age 124—the oldest known man in our era. He witnessed the fall of Quebec [Montreal?] at age 12; came to this country at the close of the Revolutionary War; was a member of the Lewis and Clark expedition, although he was not recorded in their journals.

We have the Rev. Father Donnelly to thank for the following charming vignette of the social life of the French at Kawsmouth:

They were a very sociable people—they had their innocent balls and dances, especially in winter. They got up their social assemblies on a novel but simple plan of their own. A select committee waited upon some settler and informed him that a dancing party would visit his place on a certain evening. The party waited upon was reminded that his friends expected that he would have the indispensable *pot de bouillon* prepared for his guests; but what was this *pot de bouillon?* It was a rich, palatable soup, cooked in a large pot, composed of chickens, wild fowl, venison, and sometimes slices of buffalo meat, to all of which were added a few handfuls of corn meal, with seasoning of small pepper, etc. The soup was quaffed from gourds, cups, dishes, etc.

Blanche Chouteau told me several times that at the French gatherings when she was a young girl, there were always "jars" on the table. I did not understand them to have been used for wine, and Father Donnelly's description of the *pot de bouillon* leads me to believe that these "jars" were used to "quaff" the bouillon. Father Donnelly continues:

Messrs. Joe and Peter Revard [Rivard] were the parish fiddlers—two respectable brothers. All went to the ball—men and women, young and old, and all danced. It seems to me that some of your readers would like to ask "did the beaux escort the belles to the ballroom, as they do in our polished times?" Not a bit of it. "How, then?" Why, the belles went, and returned too, by the side of their own affectionate mothers. Not only that, but the daughters took their seats in the ballroom itself beside their mothers, and at the end of every dance the beau restored his partner to the same secure place. This, too, is the proper etiquette among the old French themselves in "La Belle France." A most respectable gentleman, Mr. Northrup, informed me that he attended these parties, that he never witnessed anywhere such real politeness, such guarded deportment, and such genuine, amiable, refined enjoyment, as he witnessed among the old French (Creoles) of Westport Landing, at their winter balls and reunions. The strictest decorum, decency and politeness always prevailed.

This, then, was a true *danse de jeune filles,* a tradition carried on in New Orleans to this day, and a delightfully fitting and decorous precursor of today's Jewel Ball. Father Donnelly concludes:

> There was no liquor drank, no boisterous talk, no unbecoming word or act seen among them. All were happy; all danced; all partook of the bouillon. There were no quarrels, no contentions and no scandals among them, nor thefts, nor wrongs, nor impudicity, no adulteries, nor injustice, nor slanders, nor deceit.

Father Donnelly once wrote that on winter evenings he could stand on the west bluffs and hear the laughter and fiddle music drifting up from the French, whose balls were held at the homes of the arpent strip habitants in the French Bottoms. Aside from the fiddle music and the singing, we know little of the development of the musical arts in Creole Kansas City—perhaps because there is very little to know. Berenice Chouteau's family, the Menards, sent her a spinet to put in her new home, built after the 1826 flood.

The commerce carried on at Chez les Canses or Chouteau's was rather unique. A knowledgeable writer states:

The trade of this period was peculiar. It was chiefly an exchange of commodities. The Indian brought his ponies and pelts, and the fruits of the chase; the trapper brought his furs, and both were exchanged, not for money, for neither Indian or trapper had use for that, but for supplies—blankets, trinkets, groceries, flour, salt and whiskey—everything received here was brought by the boats, even flour, bacon and corn, which the country now produces so abundantly, were brought from eastern Missouri and Illinois, and merchants had to lay in a stock in the fall to last the community, and the trade, until the boats brought more in the spring.

Ted Brown in his book on early-day Kansas City, quotes another source as follows:

The Canadian-French were making more than a living feeding and rooming the hunters and trappers and selling garden products to the fur boats and to men passing in skiffs. . . . Nature had made a good landing place. [Buyers] would go to the Canadian squatters for potatoes, chickens and prairie birds and sometimes make contracts for a regular supply.

The large bateaux or pirogues used by the Chouteaus to transport trade goods upriver and furs down were interesting. The larger ones were up to 75 feet long and built like a ship, with a keel and ribs, and occasionally decked over. They were ten to twelve feet wide and about six feet from keel to deck. One of these monsters was taken about a hundred miles up the Kaw in the early 1800s and created quite a sensation. The Indians came from miles around to see the immense "canoe."

I have always felt that one of the heros of this piece should be Gabriel Prudhomme, but until recently I knew little more than his name. However, in early 1979, the knowledgeable ladies at the Missouri Valley Room introduced me to the 1974 manuscript of two chapters of a projected book by Philip A.

Gambone which supplied some of the missing pieces. Prudhomme was not a common name in upper Louisiana, the only
one of whom any record appears being Pierre Prudhomme
who accompanied La Salle and Tonty down the Mississippi in
1682 and became the commandant of a little log post named
Fort Prudhomme near present Memphis. La Salle gave him a
land grant 44 arpents square on the Illinois River in 1683.
Gabriel may have been a descendant of Pierre. It seems that
Prudhomme was one of the early-day boosters of Kansas City.
Gambone says that the early French were parochial and
content to live to themselves, not seeing the bigger vision
which Kawsmouth offered. "A few however, did catch the
town-making spirit. Gabriel Prudhomme, a blacksmith at the
Kansa Agency, according to one of his descendants, became so
enamored of this inland empire he determined to colonize it
and set up a trading post." He promptly suited his actions to
the thought. According to Gambone, "Gabriel Prudhomme
was granted a license in 1830 to operate a grocery store, and
this may be the 'Frenchman's store' which was standing near
the landing in 1838." He also notes that "The French Creole
Gabriel Prudhomme . . . was granted a license for the operation of a tavern in 1831, but it is not known whether this was
ever built at Kansas City." Perhaps others among the French
resented his near monopoly [his farm blanketed almost the
entire Kansas City of that day] of the grocery and tavern
business, and felt he was too much of a "wheeler-dealer."

His son, Gabriel, Jr., is said to have accompanied the famous
Father Pierre-Jean De Smet on some of his travels. Gabriel, Sr.,
received a land patent on February 1, 1831. Gabriel Prudhomme (spelled "Predom" in the land patent) died an
untimely death in something of a free-for-all among the
French in November, 1831. William Mulkey, an old-timer,
described it years later: "The family had hard luck. Old Mr.
Prudhomme was shot in a free fight in 1829 [1831?] by some
fellow Canadians. It was a fierce brawl and happened where
the gas works now stand. When the fight was over there were

many wounds and much blood spilt, and Prudhomme lay on the ground, still and dead. The murderer was never discovered. Mrs. Prudhomme [nee Susan Kris] reared her seven children . . . The boys went to the mountains as trappers and traders." The girls married, and some of their descendants still live in Kansas City. Much litigation plagued the Prudhomme estate, and it was years before the family realized anything from their property. But it was on Gabriel's original 114 acres that François Chouteau relocated his warehouse after he was flooded out in 1826, and Kansas City simply spread out from there over Prudhomme's farm.

The pattern old Kansas City took is interesting. North of Sixth Street (I-70), in the "old town" or River Quay area of small blocks and narrow streets, the streets parallel the river (diagonally, northwest-southeast) in the old-world fashion, because that's the way Chouteau's warehouse and the river wharves were oriented. South of Sixth Street the streets follow the strict American east-west survey. Seventh, Eighth, and Ninth streets are an interesting transition zone, the blocks still being smaller and the streets narrower, but laid out strictly by the compass east-west (except for Delaware which was permitted to straggle diagonally from Gabriel Prudhomme's old store or tavern on the Quay up to Ninth and Main, until very recently). Kansas City's old "city square" (now the City Market) is therefore laid out on the bias, since it was part of the "old town."

Creole Kansas City actually had another name—whether given in jest or pique I do not know—but it was a hilarious sobriquet used by the Catholic priest, Father Roux, in a letter written to Bishop Rosati of St. Louis in 1833. First a bit of background on the St. Louis French settlements. When St. Louis was founded, it bought all of its flour from well-established Ste. Genevieve, whose residents promptly dubbed the upstart village "Pain Court," i.e., short of bread. St. Louis retaliated by dubbing Ste. Genevieve "Misere," i.e., miserable, in the sense of bad living conditions. But at the bottom of the pecking order—the real pits—was Carondelet. The residents were so poor that in that day of a barter economy and socializing (which required an exchange of small gifts) they never had anything to exchange or give—and hence their town was called by the other two "Vide Poche," i.e., empty pocket.

This sets the stage for Father Roux, late of Paris and St. Louis (where he was associated with the good life at the cathedral). His term for his new ragtag little Creole parish at present Kansas City was "Nouveau Vide Poche," *New Empty Pocket*! This name tells volumes about the settlement and was no doubt fully warranted by the facts. Father Roux's bon mot was the ultimate put-down for the struggling little Creole parish, but he became its devoted priest.

What did French-speaking Creole Kansas City look like? Perhaps no one can improve on Father Roux's characterization of "Nouveau Vide Poche." But a somewhat more definitive treatment is provided in Philip Gambone's projected book on early Kansas City architecture. In it, he suggests that "the type of structures that François [Chouteau] and his companions built must have had analogues in earlier French colonial building throughout the Mississippi Valley and Canada . . . we should . . . look . . . at the (French) colonial and Creole architecture which developed during this era." Chapter II of Gambone's book is to be entitled "Log Construction Among the French Creoles." In his manuscript he notes that French construction ranged from Chouteau's rather substantial 1826 warehouse (Gambone says it was probably *poteaux en terre*, posts in the ground, since that method allowed an oversize building exceeding standard lumber lengths) to Creole squatters' shacks of loose logs and skins to some putative French brick structures of later years (two 1840 Frenchmen were brickmakers and two were bricklayers, and apparently made the first brick structures in Kansas City which were the brick chimneys on the Catholic church and parsonage). Gambone says that Father Point's 1840 map of French Kansas City homes does not give sufficient architectural detail to delineate the type of construction. He never quite reaches the conclusion (and he appears to have read *all* the sources) that private dwelling house construction in Creole Kansas City was of the standard French *poteaux en terre* with Norman roof trusses (still in existence in Ste. Genevieve) and whitewashed interior/exterior over stuccoed or plastered walls. The closest the primary sources come is a reference to a *poteaux en terre* fence of oak pickets around the cemetery (a French habitant fence) and references to "whitewashed" or "white" houses. The cemetery fence shows up clearly in Father Point's sketch of the church. An old photograph of the St. Francis Regis parsonage clearly shows the remains of whitewashed plaster on the chimney.

With the benefit of early eyewitness reports, Father Point's 1840 pictures of the old French church buildings and lot, his map, and the early real estate records, we can produce a fairly accurate facsimile of early-day Kansas City when it was a French enclave. Joseph Robidoux and Grand Louis Bertholet were purely trappers and, when they were contemporaries here in 1798-1799, probably had little more than a lean-to made of brush or an overturned bateau and caches in the ground for stored goods and furs. The same is true of the trapper-farmers who were situated between Randolph Bluffs and Fort Osage in the first decade of the 1800s, and probably also of Jaçques Fournais and his associates who came in 1815, since they did subsistence trapping and farming and owned no properties worthy of noting by contemporary travelers. The Chouteaus' post, of course, was built on the river to the northeast of downtown Kansas City. But when the first eight French-Indian families came down the Missouri in 1831, Kansas City began to assume some of its present-day configuration.

In the West Bottoms along the then Turkey Creek, there were the Trembles, Benjamin Lagautherie and probably his father-in-law, and, soon after, the Philiberts, Turgeons, Etues, Prudhommes, Edouards, Bowirds and others. Along the Missouri River frontage (from about the foot of Broadway to the foot of Grand, and then sparsely on to the present Paseo

Bridge) were the Bertholets, Compvilles, Magrithes, and the widows Chouteau and Rivard. Up on the bluffs was the *centre de la ville*, consisting of the little Catholic church of St. Francis Regis and its parsonage. Around the church were the homes of the Clement Lesserts, Bellemeres, Carboneaus, Du Lauriers, Vertifeuilles, La Libertes, Rivards, and a few others. It was the more affluent group of these up-town French families nestled near the church who first put the "quality" in Quality Hill. The old farmers in the French Bottoms along Turkey Creek particularly (but also along the Missouri) laid out their farms so as to allow for a depth back from the waterfront (irrespective of the width) of up to the equivalent of ten to forty arpents, the usual "settlers' tract" in French-American communities. The width of their front-footage on the water, on the other hand, could vary from one-half to several arpents. Several of the farmers in the French Bottoms cleared their strips of land, and their fields could be seen from the west bluffs.

Father Point has provided us with a picture of the little log church of St. Francis Regis and its smaller adjoining parsonage (used as the first church) on the same general property where the Cathedral of the Immaculate Conception is now situated. The church had a steeple and in it a belfry, but the bell (later given to St. Teresa's Academy) was actually suspended atop a pole outside the church. Through great good fortune, the very same church bell which tolled the services held by the French in St. Francis Regis Church (the same one pictured in Father Point's sketch of the church) has been carefully preserved by St. Teresa's Academy (oldest girls' school in Kansas City) and is still in active use there to mark special occasions. The bell is about 14 inches high, heavy, apparently made of cast iron, and does not appear to bear any inscription. In still has a beautiful tone. The school, which moved to its present location south of the Plaza in the early 1900s, even has one of the bricks from the old structure downtown, presumably one of the chimney bricks made by the French brickmakers. In addition to the bell, there was entrusted to St. Teresa's care a small well-worn

Original bell of St. Francis Regis Church now in St. Teresa's Academy.

silver chalice from Father Donnelly, which may have been used at St. Francis Regis Church, bearing a Latin inscription and the date 1688. There was a small cross on the far (west) end of the church gable. Back of the church, behind the picket fence, a large cross (actually erected on Father Point's last day in Kansas City) appears in the picture, and this was to become the old French cemetery (from which 1,400 interments were later transferred to St. Mary's Cemetery). Services were held at the church in French, using French Bibles, French songs, and a French catechism booklet (still in existence!). Father Point said that:

> By dint of a little industry, many little gifts, given to me in Louisiana, became ornaments, pictures, statues and even a monstrance, so that by Christmas (1840) this little chapel enjoyed all the services which are available in a big city church.

The little church seems to have had mullioned *glass* windows—probably the first and for a long time probably the only glass windows in Kansas City.

As the little French parish grew, some of the amenities were added. The Chouteau warehouse became more than a rendezvous for bachelor trappers and added merchandise for the local families. Most transactions were probably by the barter system, however. The Roys and Rivards started a ferry across the Missouri. The brickyard opened. Mr. Prudhomme opened his store and tavern. The girls' school was founded (lessons in French). And the Chouteaus and Turgeons imported their spinets!

In outward appearance the French enclave east of Kawsmouth probably revealed its Gallic nature to the discerning eye. The first thing to greet the traveler coming upriver would have been the largish Chouteau warehouse, with its French *poteaux en terre* log construction, numerous outbuildings, and large bateaux. Houses may or may not have had hip roofs, but some of them did have whitewashed mud chimneys and habitant stake fences as in St. Louis, and their narrow little strip fields extending inland from the river and Turkey Creek would have told a visitor from the St. Lawrence that he was among his countrymen. There is no indication that any of the structures in Kansas City (except the church) had glass windows. The usual practice in the habitant cabins was to use heavy paper saturated with bear grease, which let in the light but excluded the elements. Some cabins may have had thatched roofs. One of the earliest pictures of Kansas City shows the typical French provincial mode of transportation, a two-wheeled charette, on the quay. Of course in the early period there were no streets or roads. Father Point's 1840 map shows three trails leading down to the river, the principal one going past the church. Eventually Madame Chouteau would build her fine home, somewhat after the French fashion, at Third and Grand, rivaling Robidoux's homes in St. Joseph and the two Chouteau mansions and Joseph Robidoux' pere's, home in St. Louis.

Is it still possible today to envision what the habitant of French-speaking Chez les Canses or Chouteau's saw when he looked around him in, say, 1840? Yes, it is, with a little imagination. A good vantage point is the little traffic circle and overlook just to the west of Hereford Road near the intersection of Eleventh and Jefferson streets. As you face east toward the Catholic cathedral (toward the east side of the original 40-arpent church plot) the little French cemetery would have been about in front of you, and further east of it, beyond a picket fence, the log Church of St. Francis Regis and its parsonage. To your right, beyond the church were the cabins of Bellemere and Clement Lessert, on the main trail which ran in front of and south beyond the church. To your left running down the same road toward the river were several other cabin homes and the river ferry run by the Roys and Rivards, and out of sight to the east along the riverbank were other homes and eventually the Chouteau warehouse. Turn around and look to the west out over the bottom land and you see the site of the arpent strip clearings and the cabins of the farmers who lived in the old French Bottoms, a name still current in Kansas City (whenever its more current equivalent, the Central Industrial District, is not used).

It is difficult for us to realize today how thoroughly French Kansas City, and all of mid-America, was in earlier years. By way of illustration, when Lafayette visited St. Louis in 1825, that city was still predominantly French. The Chouteaus'

Chez les Canses, which became Kansas City, was virtually 100 percent French right up to 1846, in spite of the abortive attempt to plat the Prudhomme estate land in 1838 (which was held up by litigation for eight years). In spite of gradual settlement elsewhere in the area, Kansas City remained a solidly French little enclave, the province of the Chouteaus, the Roys, Rivards, Bertholets, Etues, Turgeons, and Papins. They spoke French, held their church services in French, and sang "Cantique de Noel" at Christmas and the rousing "La Guignolle" at New Year's. Missouri was so thoroughly French at its inception that the new Missouri Constitution was printed in French (and English) and the *Missouri Reader* for school children (a sort of McGuffey's) was printed in French. There was even a doctoral thesis published in French at St. Louis as late as 1840!

A fairly complete record of the baptisms, marriages, and burials in the little French community (in Latin and occasional French) was kept by the several curés of the Church of St. Francis Regis, and these records were still extant according to an article written in about 1900. These records may still exist in the archives of the Catholic cathedral.

The French of the Illinois country (which included those at Kansas City) were so out of touch with larger events, and so pastoral in their way of life, that they had no need to concern themselves with the precise time of day and the date. They reckoned time by the sun, traded, trapped, and planted by the seasons, and kept track of the years by a unique descriptive system. The year in which a particularly bad blizzard occurred (for instance, one worse than anyone could remember) would become *l' année de pouldrerie*. The great flood of 1844 thus became *l' année de grandes eau* (or "deluge"). It was this unprecedented flood which spelled the doom of French Kansas City. Every single one of the French farmhouses in the French Bottoms along the Kaw (and on around on the Missouri River side), virtually the entire French community, was washed away without a trace remaining! A contemporaneous observer told how the French drifted away after the flood, and as the Yankee population swelled "the Frenchmen were restless, hardy people and they loved good hunting and good trading. The young men went mostly to the Rocky Mountains or to the Osage Nation, leaving the old folk and the girls behind. The old folk died and the girls married, so the family names here were lost, but there's a great deal of French blood in Kansas City, though people don't hear of it."

While they were actually latecomers on the scene at the little French village of Chez les Canses, as Kansas City was then known, the Chouteaus finally anchored the little French-speaking enclave at Kawsmouth as a lasting commercial emporium. The Chouteaus had traded here since the late 1700s, and the Osage (and their Siouan cousins the Kansa) called the new emporium Cho-To-To-Wan, Chouteau's Town. There is even a "charter" of sorts extant which dates the founding of Chouteau's Town. In the archives of the Missouri Historical Society in St. Louis there is a letter from Pierre Chouteau, Jr., to C. G. Chouteau at "Chez les Canses," i.e., at the home or village of the Kansa Indians, dated August 30, 1820 (see page xii). In his hurried letter Pierre used the abbreviation "Cans.," although in his more leisurely reminiscences he used the longer form "Canses." This was the name (i.e., Chez les Canses or Village of the Kansas) which eventually metamorphosed in English into Town of Kansas, then City of Kansas, and eventually Kansas City.

But to get back to the Chouteaus, Pierre pointed out in his letter that two Yankee trading partners, Curtis and Eley, at Kawsmouth, plus a third trader (Woods) due to arrive with a "big assortment" of goods, were about to flood the local market with merchandise, and that Curtis and Eley had suggested that they join forces with the Chouteaus in order to avoid disastrous competition. Pierre noted that such a partnership has "advantages and disadvantages" and suggested that C. G. Chouteau "consider your own interests" and also to consider "the advantages you believe one can have in that post." Such study precipitated a long-contemplated decision by the Chouteaus to overwhelm their competition by sending young François Gesseau Chouteau to establish a greatly expanded, permanent trading entrepôt the very next summer near Kawsmouth—the first large scale commercial venture in Kansas City.

François G. Chouteau and his new bride Berenice (Menard) had actually scouted out the location for the new trading emporium while on their honeymoon up the Missouri in 1819. François had been a licensed trader to the Kansa for some time. The astute Creole aristocracy which comprised the Chouteau dynasty clearly saw the long-term benefits to be gained from locating nearer the source of the Kansa beaver trade, as well as being positioned for trade up the Missouri, and across the plains to Santa Fe.

François Gesseau Chouteau was the nephew of the co-founder of St. Louis, Auguste Chouteau, who as a lad of fourteen went with Pierre Laclede (François' grandfather) in 1764 to carve the new city out of the wilderness on the Mississippi. On his mother's side, François was descended from the French military engineer, Saucier, who designed and constructed Fort Chartres, the "Louisberg of the West," south of St. Louis. Berenice's father was Col. Pierre Menard, president of the legislative council of Illinois territory which was situated at Kaskaskia, "French Capital of the West."

François sent on ahead in 1820 Louis (Grand Louis) Bertholet and five *engagés* of the American Fur Company (all French) to act as an advance cadre. Grand Louis (whom we have met previously) became a rather famous figure in early-day French Kansas City and was so-called to avoid confusion with his stepson, Petit Louis Bertholet, who also came to Kawsmouth with the Chouteaus. Grand Louis was instructed to build a cabin for François and Berenice, who were expecting their first child (he was born before they left St. Louis). A portent of things to come at Kawsmouth occurred when the Sauk Indians left a calling card by tearing down

François' and Berenice's new cabin before they even left St. Louis! But the Chouteaus were not to be deterred, and in the spring of 1821, the young couple, accompanied by thirty-five Canadian *engagés* and three servants, started upriver to their new home, obedient to Pierre Chouteau, Jr.'s mandate that they consider the "interests" and "advantages" "to be had in that post," i.e., at Chez les Canses. They landed near Randolph Bluffs, about three miles below Kawsmouth.

Permanent quarters were built of logs on the south side for the men, and then the log trading post was started near which François and Berenice would live with their infant son, Edmond. The trading post may have been the only building in Chez les Canses which was constructed of *poteaux en terre,* i.e., the method of placing upright posts (probably cedar) about three or four feet in the earth to form the perimeter walls, with Norman trusses supporting the roof. The well-reasoned basis for this view is that the trading post was the only structure which was large enough so as not to lend itself to construction with "standard" lengths of logs in the *piece-sur-piece* method of construction (i.e., the usual horizontal log cabin) evident in the few smaller structures which were still extant in later days. Six cabins were built around the post, and, this accomplished, twenty of the men returned to St. Louis.

The trading post prospered, and many furs were acquired for shipment downriver in the spring of 1822—beaver in particular, but also elk, deer, and bear. Pierre Menard Chouteau was born in the spring of 1823. In 1824 General Lafayette visited St. Louis, still almost solidly French, but François and Berenice had to forego the balls and gala celebrations in order to attend to their infant sons and growing business. In 1825 François' brothers, C. G. and Frederic, joined the Chouteau enterprises in the Kawsmouth region, and also in 1825 Louis Amede Chouteau became the third Chouteau born at Chouteau's Town or Chez les Canses. There was an abundance of peace and plenty at Kawsmouth.

But in the spring of 1826 disaster struck—as it was to strike in ever increasing fury in later years—in the form of a great flood of the Missouri and Kaw. The Chouteaus lost almost everything. The post and cabins were all swept away. The Chouteaus spent the summer rebuilding west of their first site, on higher ground. Kansas City was beginning to take shape. In autumn they could rest and sing and enjoy the *pot de bouillon* again. Spring saw a good harvest of furs sent downriver, and the birth of Louis Sylvester Chouteau—and cholera! Suffice it to say that people have been beatified for doing less than what Madame Berenice Chouteau (with four infants of her own to look after) did during this terrible plague. She nursed French and Indian alike. She personally baptized 75 Indian children during the epidemic that they might die, by her lights, in God's embrace. When the fine linens from her family in Kaskaskia ran out, she used her own wedding dress to fashion burial garments for the dead! Finally, little two-year-old Louis Amede contracted the dread disease and died. Louis Sylvester followed him. Thus went the year 1827 at Chouteau's Town.

If there were ever people "standing in the need of prayer" it was the little French enclave at Chouteau's Town in 1828. Into this receptive atmosphere strode Father Joseph Anthony Lutz, a little missionary priest with a lovely Parisian accent. He was received as a heaven-sent apostle from the famous Bishop Rosati of St. Louis, conducted services for the faithful and administered the sacraments, and on the urging of François promised to relay a request for a resident priest at Kawsmouth.

The Chouteaus' business at Chez les Canses continued to expand, as did their family. Benjamin was born in 1828, Frederick in 1831, and in 1833, Benedict.

But the year 1833 brought more than one Benedict, for at long last, Bishop Rosati had answered the prayers and pleas of the little Catholic enclave at Kawsmouth to have their own resident priest. Father Benedict Roux, another "little French priest" whose heart's desire was to be a missionary in the Indian country, had finally escaped duty as a curate at the St. Louis Cathedral and been posted to Chouteau's Town. All the little parish could muster of the faithful was twelve families. But Father Roux spoke of a church, rectory, and school. Thanks to his zeal and the Chouteaus' and others' faith these were soon to be realized, in exactly that order. The first order of business agreed to by the "charter members" of the tiny parish was the purchase (or donation) of a forty-arpent French settler's grant. On Christmas Father Roux conducted services in French and the congregation doubtless sang the old "Cantique de Noel," and the celebrants wished each other *Joyeux Noel.* Father Roux baptized children and administered other sacraments—many long delayed due to the paucity of clerical assistance in the remote little parish on the frontier. Easter 1834, like the prior Christmas, was celebrated in a private home. In vestments sewn by Berenice Chouteau, the little "black robe," Father Roux celebrated Easter service with two of Berenice's and François' sons as the altar boys. And finally, the year 1834 brought the hoped for 40-arpent church tract from Pierre La Liberte, one of the earliest French settlers. Father Roux was promised (after a long illness) a church and rectory by Berenice Chouteau. The two buildings were, in fact, built to Father Roux's specifications in 1835, although the little priest never returned to Chouteau's Town because of his health.

In the intervening years, little Benedict had died, as had an infant daughter of the Chouteaus, Odile, named after Berenice's sister. But Mary Briggitte, their first daughter, born in 1835, was healthy and happy and destined to leave a lasting progeny in Kansas City.

The Chouteaus spent several tranquil years in the mid-1830s, enjoying their thriving business—and family. The older boys were able to ride and were learning the fur-trading business from their father and uncles. François needed all the good horses he could get for himself, his brothers, the boys, and his burgeoning staff. In the spring of 1838 an Indian who had become attached to the Chouteau entourage told François that a herd of wild horses had been captured by a tribe of

Indians a considerable distance to the southwest, and they
were for sale. François lost little time setting out on horseback
with Edmond, 17, and Pierre, 15, to buy some of the horses.
After several day's travel, following roughly the route of the
Santa Fe Trail, they came to the tribe offering the horses for
sale. François bought nine horses, one a stallion, partially
broken, which François used as his mount for the return
journey. All went well until, just two days out from Chouteau's
Town, tragedy struck in the Flint Hills country. A roving band
of Indians, perhaps intent on stampeding and capturing the
mares (which were allowed to run loose), topped a rise at full
gallop and with war whoops descended on the little party.
François' pinto stallion reared, threw him, and the mares in
their terror trampled François as they ran away. François was
mortally wounded, and as he looked at his two sons had only
time to whisper to them to take good care of their mother.
Thus ended the exemplary life of the man who best deserves
the title of "founder" of Chouteau's Town—later to become
Kansas City.

But life went on at Chouteau's Town. The sons prevailed
upon Madame Berenice Chouteau, now Chouteau *veuve* or
widow Chouteau, to return here after François' funeral and
burial in St. Louis. Upon her return she found that an effort
had been made to incorporate Chouteau's Town into a city,
but it had died aborning, and the little French enclave
continued largely as before, a Gallic island amid a growing
tide of western expansion of the Yankees. Steamboats were a
regular occurrence, and the Chouteaus prospered as never
before, cashing in on the old fur trade and the new interest in
the Missouri River trade and the Santa Fe Trail. Madame
Chouteau was highly respected by all the residents of Chouteau's Town and became the patroness of the little church on
La Liberte's 40-arpent plot, which in about 1839 was named
St. Francis Regis Church (but continued for years to be known
as Chouteau's Church). In 1840 Father De Smet came to
preach and baptize, and a resident priest, Father Nicolas

Point, stayed for about a year before leaving with Father De Smet in 1840. The parish now numbered about 26 families, still virtually all French. This recounting of the history of Chouteau's Town, like the rest of this book, must end with the great flood of 1844, which substantially eradicated what was left of the old French riverfront settlement first known as Chez les Canses. But I must note that Madame Berenice Menard Chouteau, the grande dame of Kansas City, patiently built a new home at the corner of present Grand and Third streets overlooking the Missouri River, rebuilt the Chouteau warehouse, and again surmounted all obstacles to reestablish the family presence at Chouteau's Town, where she lived until her death on November 19, 1888, at the age of eighty-seven! She is much to be admired, and I commend to the reader the excellent little biography on her entitled *Light In The Early West* by Rev. J. J. Schlafly which I have used as the source for most of the information in this latter part of Chapter VIII.

The ubiquitous Father Donnelly wrote the epitaph of French Kansas City in about 1855. He said that as he stood on the west bluff and looked out over the French Bottoms, there was nothing but forest, with little clearings where the French farmers had tilled their strips so many years before. The 1844 flood had washed everything away. Now only the sound of the birds and squirrels replaced the music of the fiddles and the French songs and laughter and joie de vivre which used to emanate from the old Gallic community which once was Chez les Canses.

A note on Kansas City's neighbor to the north, St. Joseph, is also appropriate in this chapter on French settlers. Robidoux (sometimes Roubidoux) is a familiar name in early-day trapping and trading circles in the area. Joseph Robidoux probably shares with Grand Louis and Mme. Bertholet the distinction of being one of the first residents of any duration in Kansas City. He spent six months in 1799 at Kawsmouth, and set up a trading agency here. That same season he scouted out trading possibilities in the future St. Joseph area.

Joseph Robidoux, pére, was a very prominent trader in St. Louis with interests in a fur company whose members read like a who's-who of the St. Louis French. The Chouteaus were associated with the same trading company. Robidoux and his wife Catherine were pure Canadian French, Robidoux being of a Parisian family from the Fauberge St. Germaine district. The very first meeting of the General Assembly of the fledgling State of Missouri met in the Robidoux St. Louis home on December 7, 1812. Joseph Robidoux, fils, was born in St. Louis in 1783. As he grew up he learned fur trading from his father and traveled throughout the Midwest dealing with the Indians. He spoke French fluently, as well as several Indian languages.

In 1803 he set up a typical French-style trading post in what would become St. Joseph. This was not very far north of the first old Kansa grand village, but in 1803 the Kansa were located closer to Kansas City, and Robidoux's trade was with the Otoes, Iowas, and Pawnees. He erected the then standard French trading structures some of which were probably *poteaux en terre* type construction. He surrounded his establishment of dwellings and warehouses with habitant fences of *poteaux en terre,* just as the French used in St. Louis. He later built a more permanent log residence (probably a *piece-sur-piece* in the Yankee fashion) which was chinked with mud *(bousillage).* He traded his goods to the Indians for buffalo robes, deer and elk hides, and beaver, otter, mink, muskrat, raccoon, and gray and silver fox skins. The trade was for the most part taken directly to the Indian customers principally in Kansas, southern Nebraska, and the Grand River country of Missouri, Robidoux employing for this purpose as many as twenty Frenchmen. Their main items of merchandise for the Indians were beads, mirrors, and brilliant cloths. The furs and pelts thus accumulated over the winter trapping and trading season were baled and stored in the warehouse (frozen), and then shipped down the Missouri past the then Chouteau's Town to St. Louis in the spring in huge "Mackinaw" boats. Robidoux continued in this fashion for nearly three decades, always being on good terms with the Indians. The post came to be called "Robidoux's Landing" after its founder. Robidoux married Eugenie Delsille, daughter of a prominent St. Louis French family, in 1812 but she died a year later. He then married Angelique Vaudry, daughter of Antoine Vaudry and Agnes (Bourasa) Vaudry.

After it became possible to purchase land, Robidoux bought two sections near his trading post. He hired a surveyor and laid out a town site. The surveyor decided to put Robidoux's namesake saint, St. Joseph, on his plat, and thus did Robidoux's Landing become St. Joseph. The papers had to be taken all the way to St. Louis for approval and recording. The streets of Robidoux's original little French town site extended from Robidoux Street on the north to Messanie (a daughter) on the south and from the river on the west to Sixth Street on the east. The east-west streets after Robidoux Street have French names because Robidoux named them after his children: Faraon, Jules, Francis, Felix, Edmond, Charles, Sylvanie, Angelique, and Messanie. The main alley was named after his favorite negro servant Poulite (Hypoulite). The principal older downtown section of present St. Joseph now occupies this original townsite laid out by Robidoux.

Robidoux is significant to our narrative of the French in mid-America for the additional reason that houses which he constructed, clearly in the French architectural manner, are still standing in St. Joseph. These are the only French-style structures built within 100 miles of Kansas City which you can still actually *touch*! The Joseph Robidoux-Francis A. Beauvais home built in about 1840 was at 902-904 Second Street in St. Joseph and was a 15-room brick structure with eight fireplaces, built by Robidoux for his daughter Sylvanie, who married Beauvais. Alas, it was recently torn down. Robidoux Row, built by Robidoux in the 1840s at 219-225 Poulite Street, is the remaining, and beautifully restored, part of a long early-day "row-housing" project. This is the oldest dwelling structure in

St. Joseph. Joseph Robidoux died in Robidoux Row on May 27, 1868.

One can almost feel the presence of Papa Robidoux in Robidoux Row. His picture looks down from the wall, his chair is there, a French prayer book sits on a stand by the bed in the room where he died, a Robidoux family armoire stands against a wall. St. Joseph even has an annual Robidoux Festival in the fall. Perhaps Kansas City should have a Chouteau Festival to celebrate its French heritage.

Robidoux fared far better in the esteem and memory of the people of St. Joseph than did Bourgmont, the first Frenchman to map and write about the future site of Kansas City, or the Chouteaus. St. Joseph has had a Robidoux Hotel, a Robidoux School, and numerous other institutions and organizations named after Robidoux. He, of course, was the founder and longtime resident of the community and serves to illustrate the beneficent and still-felt influence of the French in this area.

Joseph Robidoux's town lots figured in an early case in the Missouri Supreme Court. It seems that a creek running through the town site (probably one of the valleys apparent in Father Point's 1840 drawing) periodically inundated the town. The townspeople took up a written subscription to pay a contractor for relocating 200 feet of the creek in a conduit, Joseph Robidoux promising two in-lots, one corner lot, and $100. Apparently the contractor selected a choice in-lot (it was Lot 2 in Block 3) or one Robidoux had promised to one of his numerous children or on which he planned one of his several buildings. Robidoux resisted and the contractor sued for specific performance. Robidoux won on a technicality, the statute of frauds, because the alleged discussion allowing the contractor to select a lot of his choice was oral and not in writing.

When Father Point, resident priest at St. Francis Regis Church in Westport (Kansas City), joined Father De Smet in his trip to the upper Missouri in 1840, he made a drawing of St. Joseph as he sailed by. The drawing depicted about two dozen structures arranged somewhat haphazardly adjacent to the river (unlike Point's map of Westport which seemed to show the houses spaced on arpent strips). The St. Joseph of that day had a church with a cross on its roof and on a knoll overlooking the village was a much larger structure which was apparently Robidoux's trading house *cum* fort. With the possible exception of the fort which gives an appearance of being palisaded, the church and almost all the houses appear to have been constructed *piece-sur-piece* in the Yankee fashion. The two exceptions were a structure with "stairstep" gabled ends like Boone's Tavern in Westport, and perhaps a house with a French hip roof. He had an agreement with the government before leaving St. Louis that he would receive the grant of his trading post and thus not be considered a trespasser in lands then claimed by the Sacs, Foxes, and Iowa. This smaller claim area was apparently included in the section which he later platted. In addition to the house lots and streets and alleys, he made provision for, and donated to the community, lots for a town hall, courthouse, and market (his *centre de la ville*) and also lots for a school and several churches.

CHAPTER IX

Lagniappe:
A Little Something Extra

ALTHOUGH THE FRENCH LEFT very little of a tangible nature which survives in Kansas City today, they did leave one very tangible legacy: their descendants. These are in the literal sense of the term the First Families of Kansas City. Interestingly enough, of the first half-dozen or so French families who are prominently mentioned in the chronicles of that era, four still have descendants living in Kansas City today. But the Chouteaus, Turgeons, Etues, and Prudhommes (who married into several prominent families) are merely the tip of the iceberg. There must be hundreds—perhaps thousands—of the descendants of the early French here. When Mildred Cox (former curatrix of the Ft. Leavenworth Museum) prepared a list of names associated over the years with the Chouteau trading post, she assembled a list of about 80 names. Many of them settled here and raised families. At the time the Chouteau Bridge was being built, 50 local members of the Chouteau and other French families signed a petition to give it the Chouteau family name. The very accurate list recently prepared for the Federal District Court in Kansas of descendants of the French-Kansa owners of the 21 land grants north of Topeka (some of whom live in Kansas City) totalled over *four hundred*! Obviously, there are many descendants of the original French settlers still living in the Kansas City area.

Unlike St. Louis and eastern Missouri, there was not a

sufficiently large and cohesive indigenous French population
here to sustain the spoken language and customs. The closest
that has come to my attention was a story told me once by
James Anderson, archivist for the Native Sons' historical
collection and an avid student of the early French history of
this city. Mr. Anderson told me that when he was much
younger, he was visiting a family of French descent in Kansas
City, Kansas, and in a back room of the house (or possibly
store) there were some very elderly men conversing in French.
He said this was a family descended from Mr. Philibert, the
interpreter/blacksmith at the Kansas Indian agency. This
encounter would not be too surprising considering the fact that
when the old French Bottoms (now West Bottoms) was
platted, which was well into the late 1800s, there was apparently still a Philibert family living there for the regular
pattern of lots was broken to accommodate two large irregular
farm tracts (perhaps the standard 40-arpent French settlers'
tracts) for the Philiberts and another French family.

But, French-speaking or not, the descendants of the old
French habitants of Chez les Canses are still very much in
evidence and have some interesting stories to tell. One of the
first families to settle in the old French Bottoms was that of
Louis Turgeon in the 1830s. My friend Cy Turgeon provided
me with several family reminiscences. His grandfather was
Louis Turgeon, from Canada, who married Margaret Prudhomme. His father told him that the grandfather spoke French
whenever he had the opportunity and conversed in French
with Cy's father. He himself did not recall much French being
spoken in the family when he was a boy. His grandfather is
buried in old St. Mary's Cemetery where so many of the old
French were interred. Cy said that family legend had it that his
grandfather Louis brought the first piano to Kansas City from
St. Louis by boat, so Mrs. Turgeon could play it. The
grandfather farmed, and years after he had retired and Kansas
City had grown to the south, he was walking with Cy's father
in the midtown area and said, "Look, there's our old barn."

Indeed it was, as the city had grown south over the Turgeon farm. I believe it was Cy who said that Gabriel Prudhomme (his maternal great-grandfather) had a store around Sixth or Seventh and Delaware which he described as the "original street" up the bluffs. This accords with the city records which show not only that Prudhomme had a store (and tavern) license, but also that Delaware was one of the Chouteau's main early routes south. Garraghan's book on the Catholic church in Kansas City has a photograph of a beautiful wooden crucifix owned by Gabriel Prudhomme which was given by his Turgeon descendants to a now-defunct museum. No one with whom I have talked among the Turgeons knows where it is now. What a treasure it would be for the earliest history of Kansas City!

Speaking of Cy Turgeon's relationship to the Prudhommes leads me to comment about that interesting family. While there seems to be no one in the male line to carry the name, there are certainly a plethora of descendants. I know and have spoken to a few of them, but I don't know any family anecdotes involving their French ancestry. With the death of Prudhomme, Sr., and the problems which Mme. Prudhomme, *veuve*, and her daughters had with litigation over the family homestead (which every entrepreneur wanted to grab to plat Kansas City on) the family went into eclipse for a while. The boys all left for the mountains after their father's murder, so that ended the name here, but the girls married into several Kansas City families. I know these families rightly pride themselves on this early Gallic connection, and my acquaintances in their families advise that the older members had considerable knowledge of the Prudhomme family history.

The Etue family is one of the very, very early French families of Kansas City. They were one of the first six French families to settle here—indeed they may have been the first to settle in the French Bottoms west of the downtown bluffs. For some reason Father Point did not show them on his 1840 map of the French community, but they may have been a little south of the map area by that later date. They are mentioned many times in the early records. Theodore Etue was a Canadian who farmed on and off in the French Bottoms. There is an Etue section in the old French quarter of St. Mary's Cemetery; as a matter of fact it *is* the French quarter, since the fine Etue family monument on a large plot is one of the most prominent there, together with two or three others.

Nell Etue, who is a great-great-granddaughter of Theodore, was kind enough to respond to my calls and letters and discuss the Etues with me. She said her "Grandpa" Etue was very French indeed, so much so that he returned to Canada (Quebec) where he spent much of his life, only returning here in his old age. She says he insisted that everyone speak French to him, and her father was fluent in French and spoke it when the grandfather was around. She particularly remembered that her grandfather would lapse into French whenever the children were naughty, and he reprimanded them. Ms. Etue remembers her grandfather sang songs in French and always went back to visit relatives in Canada over the winter and wrote letters home to Kansas City in French. When he came back in the spring, he brought lots of maple syrup! She remembers driving her grandfather and parents over to St. Mary's Cemetery to see the previously mentioned Etue plot, containing the graves of her grandfather's ancestors. She also remembers as a girl riding in a horse and wagon to Westport to see some French-speaking families (there was a "Predom," i.e., Prudhomme in Westport) and also said they had Etue family members living in Shawnee in the early days.

Blanche Chouteau at 95 was not only an articulate and lively conversationalist, but also she was one of the main inspirations for this book. Blanche was in Swope Ridge Nursing Home when I met her, and I made several return visits to talk to her. She must have been a very attractive lady in her earlier days. She had dark eyes, a slightly olive complexion, and a stately bearing. She called herself "the last of the Chouteaus," although there are still a number of members of

the Chouteau family here—some collateral relatives and several more recent arrivals from the St. Louis area. But she
accurately reflected the fact that she was probably the last of
the older generation who were directly descended from and
knew personally the first Chouteaus in Kansas City and their
St. Louis cousins. Blanche was born in Alton, Illinois, in 1864.
She married Mr. Hugo Brecklein, a druggist, and survived him
and all her family and contemporaries by a generation or two.
I knew her at age 95: she died at 102!

"Papa," as she called her father, Auguste Liguest Chouteau,
was very French. She said her father gave his name the French
pronunciation "Augoo Chooto," and she said it meant "cab-
bage water." While her father spoke French, Blanche did not
learn most of her French at home, she learned it at the
seminary that she and her sisters attended. The family were all
Catholics. Her father was born in St. Louis in 1815, and in the
mid-1800s came to Kansas City to help his uncles C. G. and
Frederic in the fur trade with the Indians (uncle François
Gesseau Chouteau had died from a fall from his horse in 1838).
Apparently Blanche made some trips to Kansas City in the
mid-1800s even though she may have stayed in Alton or gone
to school for several years after her parents came here. Her
obituary, perhaps incorrectly, said she had lived here only 66
years. In any event, she told me she came to Kansas City "as a
girl" to live. Papa told her the Indians used to love "bright
calico and beads." He used to talk to her about working with
C. G. Chouteau. Blanche remembered well "Madame (Berenice) Chouteau," the grande dame of Kansas City society—
French and otherwise. Since Blanche was 24 when Berenice
Chouteau died in 1888, they were contemporaries. Blanche
said the Chouteaus used to have "big family gatherings" with
a "big table with jars on it." Perhaps these "jars" were not for
wine but were for serving the ever-present *pot de bouillon* which
Father Donnelly said the Kansas City French always had at
their soirees. Blanche remembered a lawsuit which brought all
the Chouteaus together not many years ago, as well as the

family conclave at the opening of the Chouteau Bridge. She fondly recalled the Guinottes and especially her friend Maymie Guinotte.

Since Brigitte Chouteau married into the Guinotte family, a large number of Guinotte descendants are also Chouteau descendants. My friends in the Guinotte family say that they, too, have numerous records left by the older generations, but I have no particular anecdotes to relate. The Guinotte family still has the 200-year-old dispatch box given to François Chouteau by Pierre Chouteau, Sr. (or possibly Jr.) when François established the Chouteau post here in 1821. It is in the possession of Mr. James Guinotte of Chanute, Kansas. Also owned by Mr. Guinotte is a gilded crucifix of fairly ancient vintage. There was a wooden crucifix from St. Francis Regis Church (the original French parish church) extant here in the 1860s, but it was not described as gilded and I do not know if Mr. Guinotte's crucifix is the same one. It was a family tradition that the Guinotte girls would all attend the French Institute of Notre Dame de Sion. I remember another family tradition—having the family picture taken at the Jewel Ball gathered around their mother, Mrs. James G. Guinotte, Sr., a latter-day matriarch of Kansas City in the tradition of Berenice Chouteau.

It has been my great good fortune and pleasure to make the acquaintance, via telephone, of Mr. T. J. Dennison whose ancestor, Moyse Bellemard (or Bellemere), was not only a premier resident of French Kansas City, but also received one of the French-Kansa square-mile allotments north of Topeka. The early day Bellemard received the first tract in the French-Kansa lands and also had the second house listed on Father Point's French map of Westport in 1840. Mr. Dennison has been a leader (and is the named plaintiff) in the French-Kansa litigation seeking recompense from the U.S. government for the expropriation of the Topeka grants by squatters whose titles were illegally recognized by the state and federal governments. I call these French-Kansa the Kansas Cajuns.

Like the Acadians they had already been moved off their ancestral homes once, and the Kaw grants were little enough recompense for this traumatic relocation.

Mr. Dennison has carried on the battle started over a century ago by Kansa Chief White Plume's granddaughters, the French-speaking Gonville sisters. Mr. Dennison represents over 400 descendants of the French-Kansa owners of the 23 square miles of Kaw lands granted by the U.S. government to the French-speaking and quite thoroughly Europeanized members of the Kansa Indians. In this connection I cannot help recalling Kansas Governor Reeder's testimony in the earlier trials over the grants, that the grantees were so thoroughly French that most would be recognized by anyone as highly cultured indeed, more so than the general populace hereabouts in those rough and tumble early days. Mr. Dennison told me on the telephone that of the 400 or so remaining members of the Kansa tribe, all but about a dozen are related, in one way or another, to the original 23 grantees. About 19 of the 23 Topeka grantees have descendants represented in the class action! Among these claimants are descendants of the Bellemards, the Lesserts (both Kansas City residents for a time), and the Papins (the ferry operators in Topeka whose descendant Charles Curtiss became Vice-President of the U.S.). The Curtiss descendants now live in Maryland. One family of claimants is descended in some way from Toussaint Charbonneau and Sacajawea! Mr. Dennison said a few of the other descendants now live in Kansas City, a couple live in Wichita and Topeka, and many live in Oklahoma. Mr. Dennison lives in Ponca City. He said that a good many of the grandparents of the claimant families spoke French fluently (his grandmother did) and his own mother understood French. He does not speak French himself but recognized it when it was spoken in his family in earlier years. Since Mr. Dennison represented my only opportunity so far to speak to a descendant of the Kansa Indians, the namesake tribe of Kansas City and the State of Kansas, I asked him if he knew if anyone representing the Kansa still had any of the Bourbon fleur-de-lis flags presented to the grand chiefs of the Kansa villages or any other artifacts or documents from the French period. He said no; that there were only the French family names, language, and patrimony that they are trying to preserve, represented by the French-Kansa land grants. Their only "sin" was that they spoke French (in some cases exclusively so), were by and large absentee owners, and had just a touch of Indian blood, which made it ever so much easier for everyone to rationalize the dispossession of their exceedingly well situated and valuable lands.

The lineage of the modern-day pastors of "Chouteau's Church" (now the Cathederal of the Immaculate Conception) vis-a-vis the early-day French priests of the parish is, of course, spiritual rather than temporal. But the late Msgr. Bernard Koenig was the direct successor of that dedicated handful of young "black robes" who brought the sacraments to this little Gallic enclave in the first years of the last century. Monsignor Koenig and I looked through my copy of the journal of his predecessor, Fr. Nicolas Point. We looked at his 1840 map of Westport (the old literal "West Port" on the river, not the present one further inland) with its French notations and talked about some of the old French families listed by Father Point. Some of them still attended the cathedral not many years back, many were still active here and there in the diocese, and, of course, married names may obscure quite a number of present-day French descendants. When I showed Monsignor Koenig the 1840 sketch Father Point had made of the buildings and grounds of the first church here, St. Francis Regis, on land acquired by Father Roux in 1834, the monsignor immediately recognized the 1840 parsonage as the same building as the *original church* of St. Francis Regis. He took me into the rectory dining room to show me a beautiful full-color painting of the church as it was when it was the only building on the church lot. There was the little log church with its chimneys at either end, its two doors, the big tree behind it, the

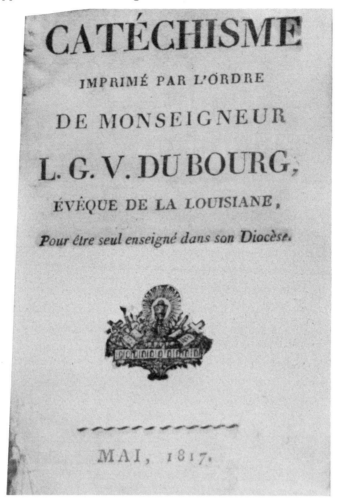

CATÉCHISME

IMPRIMÉ PAR L'ÓRDRE

DE MONSEIGNEUR

L. G. V. DU BOURG,

ÉVÊQUE DE LA LOUISIANE,

Pour être seul enseigné dans son Diocèse.

MAI, 1817.

Title page of French catechism used at St. Francis Regis Church. Courtesy Catholic Diocese of Kansas City-St. Joseph.

large cross to the left (south?), and behind all the cemetery. Whoever made the painting had a great deal of accurate historical information. After the parishioners built the "new" church, the old church building was used as a parsonage and was reputed to be very uncomfortable and drafty.

I mentioned to Monsignor Koenig that the bell of St. Francis Regis had been given by one of the French priests to the girls' school founded by the French and said I wondered what had become of it. He reminded me that the school was St. Teresa's and that it had been founded by the Sisters of St. Joseph of Carondelet who also founded Kansas City's first hospital (St. Joseph's) at Seventh and Pennsylvania.

Monsignor Koenig easily recognized the names of his early French predecessors, Fathers Roux, Lutz, and Point, and he was well-acquainted with the distinguished career of Bishop Rosati of St. Louis, who sent them here. I continued my delightful discussions at the cathedral rectory on a later visit with Fr. Stephen Wise, the unofficial historian of the cathedral parish. Father Wise showed me two other paintings of the old St. Francis Regis Church and told me that Father Donnelly, the historian of the French period, had originally been buried in the crypt of the cathedral but later was reinterred in St. Mary's Cemetery. He also pointed out to me where St. Teresa's Academy (the girls' seminary), founded during the late French period, had been located. But the high point of my visit with Father Wise was when he so kindly allowed me to see and touch an actual piece of a log from old St. Francis Regis Church and, to my utter amazement and delight, an old catechism printed *in French*, used in that very church by Luis Vasquez, the French-speaking Kansa-Indian agent who was one of the earliest residents of Chez les Canses. Suffice it to say that I left with the feeling that the memory of and continuity with the old Chouteau's Church of the early French is still very much alive in the cathedral parish.

Ou sont les Francais? They are here. The Chouteaus, Etues, Turgeons, Roys, Rivards, and many others, are still in the telephone book. We have streets, a bridge, a school, and businesses named Chouteau. Fifty descendants of the pioneer Chouteau family not very long ago joined in a request to name the bridge at Randolph Point "Chouteau," and so it was. The original French names, or Anglicized versions, are still used to describe many of the islands in, and creeks bordering, the Missouri above and below Kansas City. The French still speak to us across the years through their tombstones, their birth, marriage, and death records, and in the old downtown and Quality Hill real estate records ("Quality" because Madame Chouteau and the affluent French first lived there and set the fashion). To this day some of the first families of Kansas City—many originally quite French—still attend church as did their French ancestors on the very plot of ground given by a Frenchman near where the old Chouteau's church was founded by Father Roux in 1834—now the gilt-domed Cathedral of the Immaculate Conception. And not so many years ago Kansas City still celebrated with a certain Gallic élan the Knights of Pythias parade and ball—a veritable miniature Mardi Gras.

Walk inland from what was once River Quay and notice how the orientation of the streets changes at Sixth Street (I-70). In the old River Quay area you are traversing streets whose off-beat pattern was first set over 150 years ago by Kansas City's French-speaking founder, François Chouteau, parallel to the Missouri River on the old French riverfront. The straight east-west surveyed streets of the Yankees came later. You are walking, too, on the widow Prudhomme's estate, left to her when her French-speaking husband was killed in an affair of honor. Listen to the music—on Eighteenth and Twelfth streets and more dimly now in River Quay—listen closely and you will hear the part of the beat which started with the old French military funeral bands in New Orleans, came upriver by bateau and steamboat, and along with other strains, metamorphosed into Kansas City jazz!

For Kansas City is, at river's edge, only about 700 feet above the waters of the gulf—close enough to the Mississippi and St. Louis and New Orleans and the bayous and sugar cane and King Cotton of the Louisiana French, to share their memories of *la patrie* and *l'ancien régime*. Not altogether fortuitous is the continued vitality of Notre Dame de Sion, St. Teresa's, the Alliancc Francais, and La Causerie Francais. There is much French blood yet in Kansas City, for I have talked to many of them. Many of the old names are gone, of course, and English is now their mother tongue, but here and there a girlish eye is more coquettish, and a lad more handsomely dark of hair and eye, and family memories are longer. I know—I have met them.

For Kansas City—Chouteau's, Chez les Canses—has a history nearly three hundred years old, and to those who will listen, it whispers its poignant reminders, dimly remembered, that it was once, and sometimes is still, a river town—a levee town—a Creole town—a French town.

Au revoir.

Appendix

Governor Vaudreuil's Lease of Fort Cavagnial to Deruisseau (1744)

It has been represented to us that for several years the savage nations established on the Missouri dream only of having a French fort established in their territory to protect them from the vexations of many voyageurs from Canada who would have been able in the future to cause disturbances and dissension among them, which it would have been quite difficult for us to appease and in addition to that the disorder which these voyageurs were causing daily, competing with one another by giving away their goods at very low prices, and even selling them at a loss, which would bring about the voyageurs' ruin, and also prevent commerce from increasing with the nations because of the ease which they had of satisfying their needs, which has made them up to the present time indifferent to the opportunities for the abundant hunting in the whole extent of this river. Add to this also the liberty enjoyed up to now by many vagabonds from this government and that of Canada who would frequently cause quarrels which could have had further consequences and cause the loss of many Frenchmen. This happened only two years ago to a man named Sans Peur, who was killed by the Panimahas, and to the ones named Petit Jean and Dupre, who were killed by the little Otos since that time. Therefore, in order to prevent such abuses from happening again which up to now have found their way among these nations, and in order that the

trade of this country and that of Canada may not suffer from
them, we have, with the consent of the King, granted to Mr.
Deruisseau, Seigneur en partie de l'isle Perrot, in Canada,
whose ability and integrity are known to us, the exclusive trade
of the entire Missouri River and of all its tributary streams,
subject to the conditions hereinafter enumerated for the
duration of five years, commencing the first of January, 1745,
and ending only on the 20th of May, 1750, we reserving the
right to alter, add or withdraw the conditions of this agreement, depending upon the circumstances of the time in the
future, and consequently to make such decisions as we will
deem advisable for the good of this trade and of the colony. We
give to him and to his associate full power to make use of it
immediately in order to finish the construction of the fort and
to take there all the goods fit for trade with all the nations of
the Missouri, and we instruct them to maintain concord and
peace among them, to prevent injurious practices which they
might suffer from their men or from traders to whom they have
granted special permissions, and in case of disputes and
agitations among the savages, they are expected to appease
them at their own expense. They shall expressly forbid anyone
to organize trade, or hunt along the entire river; those who
violate the rule shall suffer confiscation of their belongings and
goods, which will go to the fermiers, and a more severe penalty,
unless they have express permission from the fermiers; they
will then be free to travel and carry on transactions with
whomever they please, bearing themselves all responsibilities;
thus they will keep this trade for the number of years
mentioned above, during which time they will be required to
discover at their own cost all mines and minerals within the
range of their business, reporting their discoveries to the
commander of the post, and to penetrate from that place at the
end of the Missouri even as far as Santa Fe itself, in order to
discover the exact location of the route, and in order to be able
later to establish trade easily with the Spaniards, and also to
increase on that river the trade of beavers, martens, peckans,

and other fine furs for the use of Canada, (which will probably find infinitely more advantages in such discoveries even more than this colony), all mentioned fine furs obtained from this trade being reserved for Canada, and for her trade, particularly the beaver, in order that the Company of Indies may not suffer, reserving only for the commerce of this Colony the hides of deer, roe-bucks, cows and other customary for commerce.

ARTICLE I

That he accepts the obligation of building and furnishing the fort which he began at the Kansas on the Missouri River, at the place designated by Mr. Legantois, following the plans which Mr. Bertet, commander of Illinois, has communicated on the eighteenth of December, 1743, i.e., "a fort of eighty feet on each side, surrounded by good posts, made of the best wood found in the place where the fort is located, with two bastions on the front side, and on the back side, according to the plan which has been made, twice as many stakes, and storied bastions.

"There shall be in the said fort a house for the officer designated as commander; it shall be thirty feet long and twenty feet wide, with rooms distributed according to the plan, already made, with wooden separation walls, and upper and lower floors. It shall be built of posts covered with bark, with a kitchen contiguous to the building, built as a shed, covered also with bark, with a chimney as on the boussilage. . . . Also a guard house, twenty feet in length according to the plan already made, built of posts covered with mud (boussilage) the whole structure covered with bark, and a chimney in said building made with mud (boussilage) with a high and low floor of split stakes, the upper being well coated with mud on its upper side. A square powder room, ten feet on each side, from post to post, covered with a high and a low floor of split stakes. Also a house to lodge the fermiers of the post, the size of which shall be determined at their convenience. Also another house for their men, the size of which will suit them."

ARTICLE II

The said Deruisseau and his associate will be required to pay the commander of the post, for each year of the lease, a contribution of one hundred pistoles, in furs, priced according to their sale at the Illinois, beginning from the first year of their lease, at the first of January, 1745.

ARTICLE III

Moreover, they will be required to carry his (other) supplies and belongings from the Illinois to the Kans, evaluated from twelve to fifteen hundred Kgs. for each year of said lease, as a compensation for his food, which his fermiers will not be required to provide, as had been previously decided, their only obligation being to furnish his table with venison available in each particular season.

ARTICLE IV

These fermiers will be required also to feed the garrison of the post at their own expense, depending upon the circumstances, with the food available, i.e., one half of a barrel of corn each month per man, and one half pound of venison each day, or if such meat be lacking, bear oil or fat mixed in the right proportions.

ARTICLE V

These fermiers shall also have the duty of providing the soldiers of the garrison with transportation for their dry goods and their clothing.

ARTICLE VI

As for the presents to the savages, the fermiers will be required to give them presents whenever among these nations agitation arises, which the commander of the post considers necessary to appease in order to maintain calm and concord among them, being careful however, to only give presents for essential reasons, for fear of abuses.

ARTICLE VII

When the savages shall come to see the Commander the fermiers will be required to give them presents only once for each first visit of the different nations, and in the case that they come later bringing the Commander a message pertaining to the interests of the colony, the Commander will give them some small presents in powder of vermillion, at the expense of the King, with moderations, however, and only on important occasions.

ARTICLE VIII

When a conference with the nations shall be considered the fermiers will have to provide the Commander with an interpreter understanding the Kans language; they may choose the interpreter from among their own men, but shall allow the Commander to choose and make use of the man in which he has most faith.

ARTICLE IX

They will be required to make reports to the Commanding officer in the post on the discoveries which they or others make pertaining to minerals, and also other discoveries taking place within the range of their activities during their years of exploitations.

ARTICLE X

The traders shall also be required to return, at the expiration of their leave, and in good condition, not only all the buildings mentioned above, but also all the little forts which they might build in the different villages of those nations for the safety and facility of their trade.

ARTICLE XI

They will not be permitted to give or to sell to these nations any drinks such as wine, brandy or other intoxicating liquors, directly, or with their men as intermediaries, or through traders carrying their permission, under any circumstances: he who disobeys will be subject to corporal punishment.

ARTICLE XII

These fermiers may appeal to the Commander of the Post if they are in need of soldiers from the garrison, whether it be to maintain peace among the French and safety in the posts, or to pursue fugitives . . . in the latter case they will have to pay the soldiers, in addition to the ordinary food ration, 10 francs a day per man, in local money.

ARTICLE XIII

No traveler will be allowed to hunt in the whole Missouri region except to the Tanerie; offenders are subject to confiscation of their belongings and goods which they might have for the benefit of said fermiers and to punishment, unless they have permission from the fermiers.

ARTICLE XIV

They will also appeal to the Commander of the post in case of dissension among the French or among the savage nations on the entire Missouri territory, or in case of dissolute behavior of their men towards the women, and bad talks which the travelers might give the savages.

ARTICLE XV

The Commander of the Post will do justice to them with regard to their men who do not live up to the conditions of their engagements.

ARTICLE XVI

They shall be maintained in all the territory covered by their trade by the Commander of the Post, to whom they may appeal in case of usurpation of their right by travelers who might go beyond the conditions fixed with them by the fermiers; the fermiers in this case shall support the costs of the troops granted to them for the purpose, since the King must not have anything to do with it.

ARTICLE XVII

They will be permitted to take to Canada the furs enumerated hereafter, i.e., beavers, martens, peckans, and other furs which will not be a threat to its commerce, and to bring back to this country the product of the sale, in goods fit for trade on this Missouri River. Said fermiers will be required to bring down to New Orleans all the other hides such as deer, roe-buck, cow, all of those, in short, which would be profitable to commerce in this province.

ARTICLE XVIII

These tenants shall receive, if possible, from the warehouses of the King at the Illinois, by paying, some goods which they might need; the price will be fixed each year by the commissaire ordonnateur of the colony.

ARTICLE XIX

And if the garrison is to move, the fermiers will be required to pay for the trip from the Kans to the Illinois, and from the Illinois to the Kans, their only obligation, however, being to feed the soldiers of that garrison on the supplies found at the place, and on the same basis as their own men.

ARTICLE XX

Finally, the fermiers will retain their exclusive trade for the whole duration of their lease, beginning today, without any one having power to hinder them on the entire territory covered by their trade on the Missouri and tributary rivers.

We hereby instruct Mr. Bertet, major commanding for the King at the Illinois, and also the officer commanding this Missouri post, to see to the execution of the present agreement made and in duplicate at New Orleans this eighth of August, one thousand seven hundred and forty-four.

Signed Vaudreuil

A.N. Colonies, C13A, vol. XXVIII, folios 224-232

La Guignolee (New Year's Song)

An old French song sung during the holidays, generally on the first of the New Year as a long-standing, cherished custom of the French people of Missouri and Canada, principally among the Canadian-French of St. Louis, and Kansas City.

Bon soir le et la maitresse et tout le monde du logis

Pour le premier maitre et al jour de L'annee

La Guignolee vouis nous devez

Si vous n'avez rien a nous donner dits-nous le

Nous vous demandons par grand chose une echinee

Une Echinee N'est pas bien longue, de quatre vingt-dix pied de longue.

Encore nous demandons pas grand de Grande chose

La fille ainee de la maison
Nous lui ferons fair bonnes chere
Nous lui ferons chauffer les pieds.
Nous saluons la Compangnie et la prions nous excuser
Si l'on a fait quelque folie
C'etait pour vous desennuyer une autre fois nous prendrons
    garde
Guand serra temps dy revenir

First (French) Families of Kansas City

A list of the old French names at Chez les Canses or
Chouteau's:

Bainville	Chosses	Godier
Barada	Chouteau	Gonville
Beauvais	Christian	Gouin
Becquet	Ciorta	Grand
Bellanger	Coil	Gray
Bellemard	Compville	Henri
(Bellemere)	Crete	Lacoate
Benoist	Crevieur	Lagautherie
Bernard	Curtis	Lajeunesse
Bertholet	Delorier	Laliberte
Bertrand	DeYeager	Latulippe
Bien	Duquette	Le Duc
Blanchet	Dupuy	Lemoine
Boisvere	Edonard	Le Sage
Bouset	Etue	Lessert
Bowird	Ferrier	Levantieur
Brisson	Fontenelle	Lievaux
Brousseau	Fournais	Magrithe
Cadoret	Gaudy	Mangeot (Mangeon)
Cadron (Chardon)	Gendron	Martin
Carbonneau	Gerber	Mercier
Chalifaux	Gourier	Membleau
Champagne	Gigiore	Montordeau

Morin
Papin
Perialt (Perriault)
Petelle
Philibert
Pinsonneau
Prieu
Prudhomme
Ravalet

Rivard
Robidoux
Roy
Seria
Silver
Tayeu
Terrier
Tremble
Tolliver

Turgeon
Uneau
Valle
Vasquez
Vertifeuille
Vieux
Youcham

Bibliography

The writer of a book such as this that seeks historical accuracy, yet is for popular rather than technical consumption, has a hard choice to make. He must decide whether to irritate the non-technical reader with voluminous footnotes, or to irritate the technical reader by having no (or too few) footnotes. The press of legal business and the type of readership at which this book is directed provide my excuse for deleting regular footnotes (which *do* appear in certain chapters heretofore published as articles in historical or legal journals) and appending general source lists for each chapter below. The Missouri Valley Room at the Kansas City Public Library will have my complete source notes.

CHAPTER I

The principal sources are: C. W. Butterfield, *History of the Discovery of the Northwest by John Nicolet in 1634,* Chapter IX, Robert Clarke and Co., Cincinnati, 1881; W. J. Eccles, *Canada Under Louis XIV 1663-1701* (The Canadian Century Series), McClelland and Stewart Limited, London, New York, Oxford University Press 1964; *The Jesuit Relations and Allied Documents*, Vol. 59; N. Thevenot, *Recuil de Voyages,* Paris, 1681; Francis Borgia Steck, *Marquette Legends,* Pageant Press, Inc., New York, 1960; G. Gravier et Cie, *Etude Sur Une Carte Inconnue,* Paris, Maisonneuve, 1880. For the Radisson voyage, see A. T. Adams, Ed., *The Explorations of Pierre Esperit Radisson,* Ross and Haines, Inc., Minneapolis, Minnesota, 1961. A much more definitive book on Radisson and Groseilliers was about to be published when I wrote my manuscript and should now be available to the interested reader. A few citations are from Margry, *Decouvertes,* Paris, 1879, and also *First Formation of a Chain of Posts,* Paris, 1887. The pre-1700 Spanish reports on Taos-bound Frenchmen are from A. B. Thomas, *After Coronado,* University of Oklahoma Press, Norman, 1969. The Marcel Wallenstein clipping at the end of the chapter is from *The Kansas City Times,* Thursday, January 18, 1962, p. 46. The reader who wants a complete review of the documents is referred to the *AN Colonies* series in the French Archives in Paris, to the wonderful English translations in the Thwaites series, *infra* (which should be consulted for the Lahontan journals) and to the bibliographical essay in the back of *France in America,* W. J. Eccles, Harper and Row, New York, 1972. Much of this material is in the Loudon Collection of the Huntington Library, San Marino, California. Where I have included in the text comments sufficient to identify a source, I have not duplicated that information in these source notes.

CHAPTER II

On Bourgmont, see Marcel Giraud, *Revue Historique,* "L'Exact Description de la Louisianne" (no date), Missouri Historical Society Archives; and *Histoire de la Louisiane Francaise,* Paris, 1953, and *Dictionary of American Biography,* Chas. Scribners Sons, New York, 1929; for Bourgmont's demands, Margry, *Mémoires et Documents Pour Servir a l'Histoire des Origines des Pays d'Outre-Mer, Decouvertes* (etc.), Paris, 1876, p. 316, and for his commission, Margry, *id.* at pp. 389-391. For his Comanche trip, Folmer, *Etienne Veniard de Bourgmont in the Missouri Country,* 36 *Missouri Historical Review,* pp. 279-298. Bossu's comments are all from Jean-Bernard Bossu, *Travels in the Interior of North America,* 1751-1762, Paris. There is an English translation of Bossu by Seymore Feiler, Norman, Oklahoma, 1962. The full texts of *Bourgmont's Journal* in French, and the English translations thereof, can be found in the references collected at footnote 25 in the article in XXX *Kansas Historical Quarterly* referred to in the source references to

Chapter III, *infra*. Regarding Ft. Orleans, see Marc Villiers du Terrage, *La Decouverte du Missouri et L'Histoire du Fort d' Orleans* (1673-1728), Paris, 1925, and also by Baron Villiers, "A Hitherto Unpublished Plan of Fort Orleans on the Missouri Drawn by Dumont de Montigny" in *Mid-America*, January, 1930, pp. 259-263. There are a multitude of books readily available on the Regency period and the early reign of Louis XV.

CHAPTER III

A very thorough set of footnotes to this chapter (127 in number) will be found in *Kansas Historical Quarterly*, Vol. XXX, 1964, p. 425. The principal sources are: A. P. Nasatir, *Before Lewis and Clark*, St. Louis, 1952, St. Louis Historical Document Foundation (especially for the French military reports); the *AN Colonies* series in the French National Archives (especially the C 13 A section regarding Portneuf and his wife); Pierre Margry, *Decouvertes* etc., Paris, 1876; Guy Fregault, *Le Grand Marquis*, Fides, Montreal, 1952; Pease and Jennison, *Illinois on the Eve of the Seven Years War 1747-1755*, Collections of the Illinois State Historical Library, Springfield, Vol. 29, 1940. On the Kansa Indians, see William E. Unrau, *The Kansa Indians*, University of Oklahoma Press, Norman, Okla., 1971.

CHAPTER IV

A complete set of footnotes is also available for this chapter. See *U.M.K.C. Law Review*, Vol. XXXIII, No. 2, Summer 1965, pp. 222-241. The sources are so scattered that no general reference to one or even to half a dozen of them would be meaningful here.

CHAPTER V

The best general source (and more complete than the list in my text) for the traders licensed during each given year and their comings and goings is "Kansas Before 1854: A Revised Annals," compiled by Louise Barry and published serially in numerous editions of the *Kansas Historical Quarterly*. These have been collected in book form and published by the Kansas State Historical Society. Nasatir's *Before Lewis and Clark* cited *supra* in the sources to Chapter III is a good source, as is Jackson's *Lewis and Clark Letters, infra,* Chapter VI and they are also organized chronologically. Also see Houck, *History of Missouri,* Chicago, R. Donnelly and Sons, 1908; Abel, *Tabeau's Narrative,* 1939, pp. 5, 6; Nasatir, "Formation of the Missouri Company," *Missouri Historical Review,* XXV, 1930, pp. 3-15; and, regarding Auguste Chouteau see the remarkably able book *The Osages* by Oxford graduate John Joseph Mathews (an Osage), Norman, Oklahoma Press, pp. 241-249. The two best general works on the fur traders are cited in the text. A good source and colorful treatment of this era is R. G. Cleland, *This Reckless Breed of Men—The Trappers and Fur Traders of the Southwest,* New York, 1950, Alfred A. Knopf and Co., pp. 14, 15 (this from the delightful library *cum* museum in Taos). For an excellent discussion not only of the fur trade but of general commercial trade in upper Louisiana, see N. M. Surrey, *The Commerce of Louisiana During the French Régime, 1699-1763,* Longmans, Green and Co., New York, 1916, especially Chapters XVII, XVIII and XIX. *The New Encyclopaedia Britannica,* 15th Edition, has useful information on beaver life and pelts.

CHAPTER VI

The materials used in this chapter are: *Letters of the Lewis and Clark Expedition,* with related documents 1783-1854, Donald Jackson, Editor, University of Illinois Press, Urbana, 1962; *Original Journals of the Lewis and Clark Expedition 1804-1806,* R. G. Thwaites, Ed., New York, Dodd Mead and Co., 1904, Vol. I; O. Skarsten, *George Drouillard,* The Arthur H. Clark Co., Glendale, California, 1964; Gordon Speck, *Breeds and Half Breeds,* Clarkson N. Potter, Inc., New York, 1969, pp. 79-148 (also from the Taos library). Just so no reader can possibly miss it, I repeat here the text reference to Anna Lee Waldo's *Sacajawea,* Avon Books, New York, 1979. James Michener's *Centennial,* Random House, New York, 1974, a tale he hangs on the life of the Frenchman Pasquinel, while it is wine from many vineyards, like Chateauneuf du Pape, is also very good.

CHAPTER VII

For a very readable history of the Kansa, with a discussion (p. 34 *et seq.*) of the "Half-breed" land grants, see William E. Unrau, *The Kansa Indians,* University of Oklahoma Press, Norman, Oklahoma, 1971. Unrau notes, p. 127, that as late as the mid-1830s the Kansa were still so thoroughly French that they could only deal through *French* interpreters! See also Anna H. Abel, "Indian Reservations in Kansas and the Extinguishment of their Title," *Kansas Historical Quarterly,* Vol. 8, 1903-1904. For some of the interminable legislation for, and litigation by, the French-Kansa, see *Brown and Brown* v. *Belmarde,* 3 Kansas 41, 1864; *Robert S. Stephens* v. *Victoria (Gonville) Smith,* 77 U.S. 933, 1869; 7 *U.S. Statutes at Large,* pp. 244-247; *Revised Indian Treaties,* pp. 410-414; 12 *U.S. Statutes at Large,* p. 21; 12 *U.S. Statutes at Large* 628; *Kansas State Historical Collections,* Vol. 5, pp. 225-234. The last mentioned article notes that the first Territorial Governor of Kansas, Andrew H. Reeder, was removed from office for alleged speculation in Kaw half-breed lands! The quotations throughout the text are, of course, from Longfellow's "Evangeline."

CHAPTER VIII

Chittenden's description of the Creoles is from Hiram M. Chittenden, *The American Fur Trade of the Far West,* 1954, Academic Reprints, Stanford, California, Vol. 1, p. 107. Fr. Point's "Plan de Westport" map is in *Wilderness Kingdom,* Holt, Rinehart and Winston, New York, 1967, Loyola University Press, p. 29. Fr. Donnelly's story about Madame Grandlouis is from the article "The Female Voyageur" in the St. Louis Missouri *Republican* of December 9, 1872. A corroborating article about Madame Grandlouis appeared in the Kansas City *Journal* on February 5, 1922. Most of the rest of Fr. Donnelly's remarks are from his reminiscences which I believe are all collected in *The Life of Fr. Bernard Donnelly,* Grimes-Joyce, Kansas City, 1921, and all of his story about Jacques Fournais is from the Westport Historical *Quarterly,* Vol. II, No.

3, November 1966, pp. 16-20. (The reader might also enjoy the article on the baptismal and marriage records of the old French families at pp. 9-15 of the same edition.) The several quotations from the diary of Prince Paul of Wurttemberg are from Louis Barry's *The Beginning of the West,* Kansas State Historical Society, Topeka, 1972, pp. 99-111. Philip A. Gambone's partial manuscript for his projected book, *Centropolis Revisited,* dated 1974, is in the flat manuscript filing at the Missouri Valley Room of the Kansas City Public Library. Most of the information on Prudhomme is from Gambone's manuscript. Fr. Roux's "Noveau Vide Poche" comment is from Gambone, Chapter II, p. 25, Note 87. The source for all of the discussion of the Chouteaus in Kansas City is J. J. Schlafly, *Light in the Early West,* Benziger Bros., Inc., New York, 1959. For an in-depth study of the history of two French families who operated the ferry at "Chouteau's" see Anderson, J. "The Roys and Rivards at 'Chouteau's'," Missouri Historical Society Bulletin, Vol. 4, July, 1948, p. 257. The vast collection of material on the Kansas City French assembled by the late James Anderson of the Native Sons of Kansas City is on microfilm in the Missouri Valley Room of the Kansas City Public Library. It could easily be mined for a graduate thesis or two.

CHAPTER IX

This chapter is for the most part oral history, i.e., a primary source. As such it is necessarily without footnotes. I have retained my original interview notes which, if anything, are more detailed than the text.